Jacqueline Llewelyn-Bowen is a professional wedding organiser and an acclaimed spokeswoman on the subject of weddings. She has organised weddings on every budget and all over the world.

Line drawings by Laurence Llewelyn-Bowen.

# Debrett's Wedding Guide

## The Planning and Etiquette of a Modern Wedding

Jacqueline Llewelyn-Bowen

**HEADLINE**

First published in 1993
by HEADLINE BOOK PUBLISHING

This edition published in 1997 by
HEADLINE BOOK PUBLISHING

10 9 8 7 6 5 4 3

ISBN 0 7472 5664 0

Typeset by
Letterpart Limited, Reigate, Surrey

Printed and bound in Great Britain

HEADLINE BOOK PUBLISHING
A division of Hodder Headline PLC
338 Euston Road
London NW1 3BH

For Laurence and Cecile

# Contents

# Acknowledgements

The kind help of the following people is
gratefully acknowledged:

Rabbi Albert H. Friedlander      Mr Jacques Azagury
Mrs June Killion                 Miss Detta Phillips
Mrs Jennifer Demolder            Ms Zandra Rhodes
Mr Johnny Roxburgh               Mr Frank Batty
Mrs Primrose Stobbs              Mrs Sarah Hammond
Mr Nigel Rawlence                Mr William Bartholomew
Mr Freddie Meynell               Miss Hazel Lacohee
Mr Ivor Spencer                  Mr Robin Guild
Mr Jonathan Hooper               Mr Kenneth Wright
Miss Vivienne Westwood

# Introduction

The day I sat at my desk in the offices of a catering company not far from Vauxhall Bridge, slowly becoming one with the telephone, trying to persuade my sister that having fittings was fun, my mother that her guests really would like duck, my brother that as chief usher it would be helpful if he could see his way to being in England and my father that paying for it all would not be so very bad, I began to understand that organising my wedding was not going to be the simple matter I had thought.

I was already luckier than most. In the time I had spent working in catering and organising countless parties and receptions for other people, I had come to consider myself something of an expert. Little did I know at the time how very different it was to be when I was the one getting married. Suddenly there were hundreds of decisions to be made and these all seemed to depend on different people and factors to do with the wedding. I confess to finding the realisation something of a shock.

The very same day and what certainly seemed to be a hundred frustrating telephone calls later in search of any reasonable mode of transport not already booked up on our chosen date, I began to wonder whether I would get to the church at all, let alone on time, unless a fairy godmother could wave her wand. Wave it she did and so materialised a wonderful fifteen-year-old sky-blue Mercedes with white leather seats, owned and driven by a friend who lovingly called it 'the pimpmobile'. Amused by how unusual it would be for a bride to arrive at her wedding in such a strange sort of wedding car, I felt there was a certain justice in the knowledge that some other bride at some other church in Kent was benefiting from the one and only limousine in the area at the very moment astonished locals happened to see us backfire past the village shop.

And so began my real love affair with weddings. Years later, with the nuptials of countless other couples fixed firmly in my memory, the celebration of a marriage still holds a compelling fascination for me. To create a day that will remain in the memory of so many people as having surpassed their greatest expectations and sometimes their wildest dreams is always a challenge.

I do not for one moment believe that my personal experiences during my wedding were in any way exceptional. Behind all the administration and planning, in order to get everything done, is the certain knowledge of the importance of the step that you are taking and how it is likely to affect your life.

What is more worrying and harder to control is exactly how far back this consideration gets pushed as the practical matters take over. Brides and grooms do sometimes find that far from becoming emotionally closer as the wedding approaches and plans hot up for the big day, they actually spend less and less time together and communication can break down to such an extent that they start to question whether or not they should really be getting married at all. If either or both has spent the entire day trying to sort out problems to do with the wedding, it is probably the last thing they are likely to want to discuss when they do see each other.

I have immense sympathy for anyone finding it hard to come to terms with the pressures of organising a wedding. The sheer number of considerations that have to be carefully thought out and acted upon make it both advisable and necessary to start the planning of a wedding well in advance of the anticipated date. This will often mean the attention and energies of more than one family are focused upon a far off event for up to a year or more. Just because a wedding is to take place does not mean that other areas of life can or do come to a respectful halt.

Weddings are a very special type of celebration, both in our private lives and from a professional point of view. No other celebration surpasses the importance, effort and expense traditionally invested in a family wedding. The historical reasons for this are discussed in the first chapter, but the important point to make right now is that the skill needed to organise weddings is something even professionals, such as myself, spend many years learning. There is no straightforward logical reason to suppose that anyone should be expected to be able to organise a wedding. A wedding is often the largest and most important event in someone's life and it does not necessarily follow that living with this understanding and the resulting pressure should be an easy business. And while for countless generations women have traditionally assumed responsibility for organising weddings, the reasons are not founded in any biological aptitude. Why should a bride or her mother be somehow expected to carry an in-built wedding organising mechanism in their make up, that can be turned on when required?

Every bride, regardless of her personal circumstances, probably has moments when she just does not know how she is going to cope. Quite apart from the responsibility of all the organisation involved, the pressure on her personally to be the most beautiful, the most composed and the most radiant she can be will often produce the strangest physical effects. Worrying about whether or not she is going to erupt in spots on her wedding day will inevitably bring them out in plenty. Some girls spend so many nights lying awake in terror dreading the day with all their might that it is a wonder they get there at all. Others lose so much weight that they are virtually unrecognisable and even invisible under the acres of satin and tulle chosen by their former selves. Indeed, even today it is a sad realisation that grooms still have little to do with the organisation of their weddings. Perhaps if they did, they would show a little more understanding of their brides and the stress they so often go through and would be able to offer a degree of support.

Weddings have the reputation of being able to turn perfectly happy families into factions versus factions and charming young women into either nasty self-important dictators or sad, weepy little creatures as a result. Family feuds are not necessary and can be avoided with small, but continued and deliberate effort on everyone's part. With careful planning and diplomatic behaviour, a wedding can take place without a single unkind word or thoughtless deed. It is only because everyone in a family places so much importance, rightly, on the wedding that they each have an opinion to give. It is a respectful and sensible bride who will give each person the chance to express their opinions, whether or not she takes the advice on offer.

Brides often feel that they are very much alone, struggling under the weight of responsibility and with no corner to call upon for help. The desperation that can result is understandable but destructive and must be avoided at all costs. There is no historical precedent to suggest that a bride should become a one-woman administration machine the moment she announces her engagement. Historically and traditionally, weddings have always been the joint effort of the bride's family and in particular her female relatives, under the supervision of her mother. Society has changed, however, and we can no longer assume either the existence, presence or constructive help of a modern bride's mother in the planning of her wedding. It is for this reason that this book is aimed very deliberately at the bride of today. I know it will have a wider readership and certainly other members of the wedding party should most definitely be encouraged to read sections relevant to them, but one thing remains certain, that whether or not there are mothers, sisters, fathers or brothers, there is always a bride.

Many millions of pounds are spent every year in the United Kingdom in search of the dream wedding. There is no doubt that weddings are expensive and the national average spent on a wedding in recent times has increased on an annual basis, as has the number of couples getting married. The Wedding Industry is a lucrative one for companies and services which operate within it and, as with any other area of life, there are those whose primary aim is to make money regardless of the service provided in return. More often than not, such people get away unchallenged. Their belief that the average wedding client will not know or expect any better is sadly often founded on truth. Knowing that a wedding is likely to be the only time a family is prepared to part with the kind of money a wedding costs, the mere mention of the word can have them adding an extra percentage of profit on to the prices quoted. There is also an argument, often expressed in retaliation to this accusation, that wedding clients are more demanding than others and give more 'trouble' to the company or individual working for them and therefore the extra cost is justifiable in the circumstances. The truth in this argument is questionable. Wedding clients, like any others, have an absolute right to expect the highest standards from those working on their behalf, and at their expense, towards what is a most important day.

Sadly, there are few ingredients in the recipe of a wedding which guarantee safety from those who will seek to take advantage of you. You have probably never organised a wedding before and this book is written for every bride faced with organising her wedding and contains a great deal of professional advice and support. I have at various points received assistance from many kind and highly respected individuals, all experts in their fields, on particular details in order to give the fullest account of exactly what is involved as you work towards your wedding day. To these contributors, colleagues and friends, I express my personal thanks.

I have never sought to justify the cost of a wedding, but to ensure that the couples and families I assist spend the money they decide to spend wisely and with the best possible effect. How much you spend must be a personal decision based upon your own financial circumstances and in the light of advice given throughout this book. By using its chapters as a step-by-step guide, and making notes as you go, you will be able to approach your wedding with confidence, knowing that you will celebrate your marriage with competence, individuality and style.

# 6 INTRODUCTION

When all is said and done and the months of hard work are over, even the most glorious wonderful wedding day is nothing but memories, but these are important to our lives. Truly happy memories shared of times past can help to overcome the difficulties we all have to face from time to time.

# The Basics

# CHAPTER 1
# Weddings in History

Few events in our personal lives provoke quite as many differences of opinion as those expressed during the planning of a wedding. Considering that a wedding is supposed to be a joyous, wonderful occasion, we must ask ourselves why the experience can so easily result in argument, confusion, exhaustion and inappropriate extravagance.

Marriage is a public rite of passage and, like birth and death, has been celebrated in different forms and different ways throughout the world, since the earliest communities grew up around small tribal settlements. The cycle of life and the fertility symbols that have for so many thousands of years been used in ceremonies of celebration hold the key to a great many wedding customs still in use all over the world today and reveal the fundamental purpose of marriage in human terms – procreation to ensure the survival of the species. Since it is in the female of the species that the potential for reproduction lies, she is a prize indeed and one that is worth protecting. Marriage has always been inextricably linked with the position of women in society.

If we are to have any understanding of how and why we celebrate marriage in the way that we do today, we must look at the past.

Weddings and the decisions which prompt them have seldom been private affairs. The search for a husband or wife for a daughter or son nearing marrying age would not have been undertaken lightly or without due consultation with other families and communities. Making a good, practical match involved a great many considerations other than whether or not the couple had ever met or actually liked each other. Physical attraction to each other would, of course, be a bonus as it would certainly help in the begetting of future generations, but it has been fairly low on the list of wedding criteria over the centuries. A satisfactory marriage would be one that either brought, or helped to keep, social stability.

Intermarriage between rival families, and at a royal level, warring nations, was far more likely to seal a lasting peace than

any amount of negotiation or treaties and, as such, became a political necessity. Royal daughters would be pledged to the sons of foreign kings at an early age and marriages by proxy were not uncommon. When the young princess was deemed mature enough to assume her adult role as queen or queen expectant to a foreign throne, it was her duty to accept the voyage to her new home, often never to see her family or country again. She was a privileged and protected hostage, but a hostage nonetheless.

In such feudal systems, the same values and principles applied throughout the echelons of society. Noble families sought to gain power and influence through the marriages of their children, and every effort would be made to secure the best possible match.

Without beauty or position, a father would need to provide an even greater incentive to persuade a man to take his daughter off his hands and dowries as a sweetener are as

ancient as marriage itself. No money and no husband would
mean a girl being sent off to a nunnery to spend her days in
contemplation of spiritual rather than earthly pleasures, so no
effort was spared in the hunt for a husband. Questions of
compatability or affection between the couple were not a
feature of marriage until relatively recently. Marriages between
young women and much older men were quite common and
indeed, for a long time actually considered ideal. The bigger
the dowry offered by her father, the bigger the fish she could
hope to catch, even if they were old, scaly and smelly.

Accepting that the boundaries of choice of husband or wife
were dictated by the need for social and financial security, it is
easier to understand how little changed over many centuries.
Until as late as 1882 in England, women were not allowed by
law to own property or money in their own right and even after
laws were passed to correct this position, only a portion of a
woman's fortune remained in her control after her marriage.
For centuries, whatever came with her, jewels, clothing, carriages, servants and all, became the property of her husband
immediately the marriage had taken place. Not surprisingly,
wealthy heiresses were vulnerable victims of trickery by dubious money-hungry husbands. Early police records detail the
notorious reputation of certain parts of London in which these
wicked, but legally binding marriages, were rife, encouraged
by sinister priests and criminal communities working together.

Queen Victoria, although a formidable monarch and one
whose colonial conquests should have been attestation enough
to her force of character, did nothing to improve either the
position of women in British society or their control over their
own lives. Quite the contrary. While working-class women and
children, often as young as three years old, were put to work in
mines and factories as cheap, slave labour, genteel Victorian
society perpetuated the myth that women were purely decorative creatures, incapable of rational thought, whose only ambi-
tion in life should be to provide a safe haven of domestic bliss
for their more than essential husbands. Young girls were
encouraged to concern themselves with beauty and the social
accomplishments needed to attract the best possible husband,
as had been the case for many hundreds of years previously.

It is no wonder that in this society of sentimental obsession
with idealised femininity, Victorian ladies found ample opportunity for exploring and reviving ancient wedding customs.

Offended beyond all measure, no doubt, by the aphrodisiac properties attributed to certain flowers and plants traditionally used as decorations for weddings for obvious reasons, alternatives would be found as emblems of 'chastity', 'hope', 'fidelity', 'innocence' and so forth. The same approach was taken with gemstones, whose fiery colours were popular with fashionable Victorian ladies and therefore could not be done without, but whose 'meaning' could not be allowed to express alternatives to 'sobriety' and 'self-control'.

Justification for the revival and, at times, perversion of the symbolism in which the Victorians, and more particularly their Georgian grandmothers, indulged can be found in the customs of the civilisations of the ancient world, especially those of Greece and Rome, the study of which had been a fashionable, intellectual pastime since the Renaissance.

Eager for precedent in ceremonial and social events, the courtly yet religious image of England's Gothic past was also a fertile source. Without the dubious connotations of Paganism, but with the equally dubious overtones of Roman Catholicism, the nineteenth-century mentality was more than able to simply take a little bit from one, a little bit from the other and blithely sweep anything unpleasant under the Savonnerie revival rug.

Both the Georgians and the Victorians were great travellers and collectors. The immense popularity of travel and avid acquisition of *objets d'art* from around the world prompted interest particularly in the Greek and Roman heroes and deities. The wealth and culture of the ancient civilisations were to be respected and aspired to, and not surprisingly by a nation itself obsessed with conquest, supremacy and Empire. Parallels were drawn and traditions revived to lend weight to the nineteenth-century British superiority over the rest of the world.

As the customs, learning and culture of these ancient civilisations were investigated and often mimicked, so too were the fashions. The sculptures and statues flooding into the houses and gardens of the wealthy offered clues to ancient hairstyles, accessories and dress and nowhere is this influence more apparent than in the style adopted by brides on their wedding day.

As a symbol of purity, the colour white is long associated with the virginal qualities of a bride. However the nineteenth-century interpretation of the significance to the ancients of

white clothing was partially distorted. The clothing on the
statues was white as the simple result of centuries of weather-
ing which faded original colour and detail which would have
been applied after the stonemason had finished his more
permanent work.

In an attempt to emulate the high-minded ideals and civilised, cultured habits of the ancients, Victorian brides adopted
white as the fashionable colour for marriage. Until then, brides
would normally have been married in their best, or Sunday
clothes, regardless of the colour. Along with the dress came
hairstyles and accessories, both jewels and flowers, in particular orange blossom which, though not native to our shores,
would have been a natural fragrant choice of any Mediterra-
nean bride. Orange blossom, like white wedding dresses and a
score of other wedding customs, revived as tributes to the
ancient world, has remained with us today in our wedding
ceremonies.

As a bride of today, the experiences you will have as you
plan your wedding will probably be very different indeed from
those of our grandmothers and even our mothers. The choices
you make will be with the benefit of education, freedom and
opportunity in a world receptive to individuality and self-
expression. No longer representative of an implicit social duty,
marriage has, certainly in the western world, become a personal rather than public decision. Though whether in two
thousand years historians will look back upon the twentieth
century and mark it as the turning point in the history of
marriage is doubtful.

Modern marriage is a lifelong partnership entered into by
two people who understand the implications of responsibility
and commitment to each other, but to deny the legacy of
thousands of years of custom and tradition is to deny the basis
upon which all human society exists. Whether celebrated in a
religious or civil ceremony, a marriage requires to be witnessed
and therein lies the crux of the matter. Even today, with our
increased sophistication and understanding of the world, more
recent wedding traditions, such as photography of the event
are based on this same fact. Early photography was not
developed as a creative medium nor originally used at weddings to provide a nostalgic memento for the bride, but as a
historical record of the event that took place, in the same way
that important marriages have been recorded for posterity in

painting for many hundreds of years.

Marriage has always been of general public interest, affecting plenty of people other than simply the bride and groom. Family involvement in decision-making for weddings does not stem from a desire to interfere or control events but from a historical and therefore justifiable tradition of responsibility and duty. Considering that for so long the future happiness of the bride and groom was probably the least important consideration of the marriage, we have, after all, come quite a long way.

# CHAPTER 2
# Etiquette

Of all the elements to be considered in planning a wedding, the question of etiquette can prove to be the most stressful. Twenty years ago, there were immutable rules; things were either right or they were wrong. Whilst this code still exists, the sections in this book will illustrate that strict adherence to rules codified over the last 300 years is no longer an essential consideration for today's bride. Understanding the rule book is, however, necessary since much of wedding etiquette is simply the provision of do's and don'ts to ensure polite considerate behaviour from wedding party and guest alike.

For such an important and, inevitably, such an expensive day, it is essential that the celebration of your marriage is both relevant and personal. A practical and well-balanced attitude to the interpretation of etiquette should without doubt be encouraged. If you want to do things a certain way going directly against the established form, it is wise to analyse your motives. If your view of certain points of etiquette is based on deeply-held opinions or feelings there is not a single person in the world who could possibly be offended, provided your approach is tempered by consideration, respect and a sense of appropriateness. Never ever consider bending the rules simply to shock or draw attention.

Etiquette, like language, cannot remain static and many conventions, though highly decorous, are now irrelevant to the way brides behave today. Never think that you cannot have your wedding cake and eat it; you can be a medieval princess for the day without compromising your individuality and achievements as a late twentieth-century woman.

As you plan your wedding, it is your choice whether to abide by the ancient wedding traditions as prescribed by etiquette or to do things in your own way. What is certain, however, is that the rules of etiquette should only be used correctly and with a certain historical understanding. Misguided or misapplied etiquette serves only to highlight the ignorance of those involved and humiliates rather than glorifies. Take note of the

rules of etiquette, understand them and then decide whether
or not to apply them.

The term 'etiquette' can be traced back to ancient French
and to the fourteenth-century verb, 'estiquer', to label, or stick
a label on something. As a verb to describe a common enough
activity, it reappears, however, and by the eighteenth century,
is in widespread use to describe the set of rules drawn up
originally in the reign of King Philip the Good of France,
governing what was and what was not acceptable behaviour at
the French Court.

Before the enormity of the impact the rules of etiquette were
to make upon the behaviour of the nobility of successive
European monarchies (for its influence was widespread), it is
very hard for us to imagine just how uncivilised life at Court
would have been. Intrigues, power struggles and constant wars
emptied coffers and left monarchs in insecure positions,
dependent on the loyalties and wealth of families who collectively had more real power than they themselves had. Etiquette
was to establish the monarch, once more, as the absolute
pinnacle of society, whose divine right as king was again
unquestioned, and demonstrated by restrictions imposed on
the behaviour of all lesser mortals.

As an exercise in French royal control, etiquette not only
survived but flourished, as successive kings added to and
improved upon restrictions governing the behaviour of their
subjects. By dividing their subjects into social groups and
imposing a different set of rules upon each, according to the
degree of nobility and position, French kings could retain an
unprecedented level of control. As long as the various social
groups at court were busy trying to score points off each other,
they could not join forces against their king. Any subject
overstepping the mark could simply be banished from court
for etiquette offences which formed a smokescreen around
their real crimes. No monarch would willingly choose to have
intrigues against him made public knowledge for fear of
looking weak or vulnerable.

So great was the continued need for control and the very
real danger should the structure of society break apart that, by
the time of the French Revolution, when it did fall apart, the
rules of etiquette were so detailed and exacting as to take a
lifetime of learning. Everything, truly everything, that was
worn, eaten, drunk, written, said and done at Court was

permitted or not on the basis of the rank and position of the subject concerned.

In setting itself apart to such an enormous extent from its people, the French monarchy ultimately signed its own death warrant and actually brought about the very opposite result to that which the rules of etiquette had been intended to achieve, but not before their influence had taken hold on other European Courts.

For many years the French monarchy had been the envy of all Europe. As a nation France was strong in battle and land-ownership, cultured in the arts and rich in economic wealth. Its geographical position at the heart of Europe and as a gateway to the then acceptable civilised world probably contributed to this reputation in no small way. The French were crusaders, conquerors and empire builders. As a language, French was more sophisticated than other European languages and as a result of successive intermarriage with other European royal houses, it became the international language used at all Courts, including our own and with the language came the rules of etiquette. It is no accident that the education of our own Royal Family should have included the study of French and that Her Majesty, the Queen is highly respected for her articulation of the language, in continuation of traditions going back several hundred years.

Court language was also the diplomatic language in which ambassadors and envoys would communicate while visiting foreign countries. We only have to look at the simplest form of invitation we send today to find the influence of traditions of etiquette established hundreds of years ago. R.S.V.P. is an abbreviation of the French, *répondez s'il vous plaît*, 'please reply'.

It is not surprising that as the centuries passed and methods of communication developed, the rules of acceptable social behaviour become modified in day-to-day living for the sake of convenience.

Diplomacy, however, is another matter entirely. Successful international relations depend, historically and continually, on the acceptance by all nations of a code of practice and behaviour, the guidelines of which are at the root of all etiquette. As a mark of respect and so as to avoid dispute or offence, positions, titles and rank have always demanded to be noted and be seen to be noted. Everyone has to play the game by the right rules or not at all.

Diplomacy continues to use the written form and abides by the etiquette of past centuries more faithfully than almost any other field of work, except perhaps royal employment. It has always dominated all forms of official or formal written communication and continues to do so, accounting for the style of invitations we still traditionally send for important social occasions and, in particular, weddings. While invitations are no longer handwritten in the way that they would at other times have been, the style of old fashioned script remains. Even the fact that formal invitations are worded in the third person gives a clue to the ancient application of etiquette laws. By referring to the host in the third person, their full title and rank is included for all to see, acknowledge and respond accordingly.

When we consider or discuss wedding etiquette, we must accept that we cannot take it out of context. Weddings are just one of the many formal social occasions at which the history of etiquette on a much grander scale has a part to play. If we accept wedding etiquette in any way at all, we are accepting marriage as the historical tradition it really is and as the social occasion it has always been.

The problems many families have in understanding wedding etiquette are explained by two factors. The first of these is that for many of us, weddings are the only times in our lives when we are particularly concerned with what is, or is not, correct behaviour and the second is how to define the correct behaviour in a contemporary light. With all the conflicting views and opinions expressed by modern culture, education and habit, how is one to unearth what was correct, what now is and how far back one is expected to go?

The answer is twofold. Firstly, traditions are there to be upheld or not, as the case may be, but they offer a wealth of enjoyment either way. Secondly, the rules of etiquette have their foundations in history as a means to ease communication and simplify social living. For 'modern wedding etiquette', we should perhaps read, 'appropriateness' instead, which is both an easier term to understand and probably more relevant to our lives today. Etiquette as a means of social control was actually always based upon what would or would not have been appropriate behaviour in context.

# CHAPTER 3
# Planning and Budgeting

## 1. The chain reaction

The organisation of any social event needs to be approached as a chain reaction and a wedding is no exception. Every decision that is made will in some way determine the outcome of the next and it is vital that you understand the likely implications of all decisions before they are made.

Choosing the form your wedding day will take is now your first consideration. Weddings are expensive and there is no point in picking a style of wedding that your financial resources will not allow you to put together properly.

Every couple getting married will have limitations of some kind to consider. Budget is often the most obvious of these, but this can be difficult to assess or know how to apply at this early stage. Geographical setting or the season of the year in which the wedding is to take place may restrict or widen the choices open for the wedding, but in any case, the limitations governing what might, or might not happen at a wedding, are the essential foundations upon which to build. Wedding day dreams often need to be compromised to logistical practicalities and it is far better that these compromises should take place early on, while decisions are still flexible and there is still time.

## 2. Appropriateness

Every wedding should be as personal as the union it celebrates. Successful weddings are those which reflect the personalities, tastes and to a certain extent, sense of humour of the families involved. Weddings are generally larger and more expensive parties than any others we hold in our lives, and of course, a tremendous amount of importance is attached to them, but they should always bear a resemblance nonetheless to the way in which a family would normally entertain its friends. Some of the traditions associated with weddings can seem old fashioned and silly if taken out of context, others make perfect sense and it is very much up to you to decide what to take from the old, what to take from the new and how much spice to add.

### 3. Shock waves

While a wedding gives brides and grooms and their families the chance to express their individuality and creativity, it is not the time to shock. By its very nature, a wedding tends to involve people from a wide variety of financial and social backgrounds and age groups and it is important to establish a common ground on which everyone present is able to enjoy themselves. Weddings which are too unusual or different can make guests feel very uncomfortable because they are not sure how they are expected to behave. Bear in mind that while you and your families will probably have spent many months planning the wedding and will be prepared for whatever festivities are planned, your guests will have little indication of the programme of events from the invitations you will have sent out and you should plan the sequence of events with them, as well as yourselves, at the forefront of your mind.

If you are planning an unusually long reception or the anticipated sequence of events may require the guests to be forewarned (for example if there is to be Scottish dancing and they will need to have soft shoes), you can consider including this information with your invitations.

### 4. Wedding guests

If you invite someone to your wedding, it should be because they are important to you and because you want them to be with you on your wedding day.

No doubt you will have given some thought to the implications of the numbers and per capita cost on the wedding budget, but will you also remember what you are asking from them? The giving and organising involved in a wedding is not the one-sided affair many families hosting the event seem to think.

Being a wedding guest is an expensive business. There is a present to buy, clothing to be bought or hired, transport and possibly accommodation, and certainly busy lives to be arranged around your plans. The average cost to a wedding guest attending a wedding could be somewhere between £50 and £150 and when you consider that a guest may well be attending several weddings in one year, it all adds up. Weekday weddings may entail taking time off work or finding a babysitter.

It is asking a great deal of a bride to try to understand that her wedding is probably just one of the many her guests will attend in the course of a season, but it is a request that needs to be made.

A wedding is not a wedding without guests. The word itself means the public celebration of a marriage and both religious and civil ceremonies call upon the guests as witnesses to the marriage. They are not simply a passive audience, but are expected to support you in your future life together and help you fulfil the solemn promises that you will have made to each other.

Out of respect for the trouble which your guests will have taken to attend your wedding, it should be your wish, as well as your responsibility, to look after them well. Of course nobody who loves and respects you would ever mind the effort required on their part to be with you on your wedding day or will ever forget how stressful and difficult weddings can be for the families involved. We all enjoy receiving wedding invitations and attending the weddings of our close friends but at the same time it is human nature to feel a little bitter and twisted when we feel that our basic needs have been ignored. Embarrassment or physical discomfort will spoil the day for everyone, including you. A roomful of grumpy malcontents will not create the wonderful atmosphere of celebration which should be the result of all your effort and expense.

Creating a sense of happy well-being in your guests is not such a difficult task and certainly, thinking about how your efforts are likely to be received goes a long way to helping you make the right decisions. But because the response of your guests will be such an essential part of your own memories of the day, it is a point we will return to time and again.

## THE GUEST'S EYE VIEW

A wedding will always involve travelling on the part of a certain contingent of guests, however small. The timing of your wedding is important to them as well as to you. The bride who thinks it is fair to expect her guests to cross half the country in time to arrive at an early morning service could not be more wrong. Nobody will disagree that it is her special day, however, unbreakfasted, unslept guests, sporting the remnants of a bad shave in the car on the way down, will not make a suitably awe-inspired audience for her magnificent entrance. So be reasonable. Give people the chance to get to your wedding composed.

By the same token, long-distance guests will need to head off for home at a reasonable hour. Receptions that go on and on with no formal leaving can cause confusion. It is a point of etiquette and one that your older guests would certainly feel duty-bound to accept, that guests do not leave a wedding reception before the bride and groom. If you are planning to stay at the reception as long as possible and dance into the night, it is as well to make sure that the groom or best man informs the guests of this during the speeches, so they are not left waiting for a formal leaving that never comes. The other option is the 'quick once round the block in the car and back again', to give those who have to set off for home the chance to say their farewells without embarrassment.

### SINE BACCHO ET CERERE, FRIGET VENUS
### (WITHOUT FOOD AND WINE, LOVE GROWS COLD)

The subject of exactly what, when and how much you are expected to provide at your reception by way of refreshment is dealt with in detail later on. Nevertheless, certain fundamental truths have to be established. Wedding receptions where food and drink are limited are usually the result of a budget crisis, which should and could have been avoided. A family may simply have invited too many guests and be forced to stretch the budget just a little too far, or they may have committed themselves unwisely to a form of reception they simply could not afford.

You cannot disinvite guests who have received an invitation, nor can you expect anyone to go a whole day on a couple of sausage rolls and a glass of sherry. There is a definite place in the world of weddings for short receptions, at which a few thoughtfully chosen things are passed around for perhaps two to three hours but such an approach must be accepted as necessarily short and sweet. Country weddings can be particularly tricky because of the lack of any other sources of food around. At least with a town wedding there are plenty of restaurants and hotels where the starving wedding guest will be able to find a meal if they leave a wedding reception fainting with hunger. In the country one is always at the mercy of pub opening hours and provisions and finding something to eat in the early hours of the morning after the frugal night before can be a big problem.

The general rule must be that the further you are expecting your guests to travel and the longer you expect them to remain at your reception, the more you will need to provide to ensure that they are well looked after.

Wedding meals are best planned to coincide with a logical mealtime. When you send your guests an invitation to your wedding, it does not include details of what you are giving them to eat and drink. A wedding service can be followed by a variety of forms of reception and the last thing you want is to find that none of your guests have the appetite to eat the five course meal you have planned because, knowing your service is to start at 3 o'clock in the afternoon, they were all expecting afternoon tea and had lunch before they came. Full meals must be planned for mealtimes and the form of any other celebration fitted in with a thought to the time of day.

## PAYING ATTENTION

Every guest attending your wedding will expect to be given their very own minute or so of your undivided attention. There will be those who you will not have seen for ages, those you may never yet have met and those who after years of love and respect will be longing to share their happiness with you.

Having a receiving line is a good way of ensuring that every guest is welcomed by the bride and groom and their families and introduced to those they do not know. Making guests feel wanted is so important.

Receiving lines are sometimes dispensed with when the bride and groom are anxious to have a very informal atmosphere to the wedding and this really is wrong. You would be unlikely to invite friends for an informal supper and not greet them somehow as they arrived. The same applies to weddings. Receiving guests does not have to be done in a regimented line-up of all the members of the bridal party with guests stiffly waiting in queues. If drinks are served to all guests on arrival, they can then start to enjoy themselves and drift, in small groups or individually towards the bride and groom and their parents to say 'hello'. What could possibly be more natural?

A strange feature of weddings is that the bride and groom take on a sort of semi-royal persona and some guests will hesitate to approach the bride in particular for fear of seeming to be monopolising her time, so the effort to speak to everyone at some point must come from the newly-weds' side. Every effort should be made to be as natural, sociable and accessible as possible if the guests are to feel part of the wedding, as they indeed should.

## 5. Cutting your cloth to suit your means

Taking all these considerations into account, you are now ready to start making informed choices. The question of who pays for what and when is a complicated one and needs some detailed discussion. It is the financial aspect of any wedding that is more likely than any other to cause trials and tribulations and a sensible bride will tread carefully along a diplomatic path from the very beginning.

You may already have come some way to understanding why historically, the costs of a wedding have traditionally been met by the bride's family. Fathers of one or more daughters are quite likely to have made contingency plans for paying for their weddings long before any engagement is announced.

Regardless of what the wedding budget might or might not afford, the gesture is a demonstration of a father's sense of duty and honour and is made out of love and respect for his daughter and should be seen as such.

A wedding is a large chunk out of anyone's housekeeping and it is a more modern approach to accept that those who are best able and willing to contribute to the costs should be allowed to do so.

Couples today are quite likely to have a joint income that matches or surpasses those of their parents in which case they may consider making some financial contribution themselves. In truth, when brides and grooms pay for their own weddings they do tend to be more realistic in their expectations and it is always a good exercise in self-discipline to ask yourself whether a particular extravagance would be so important to you if you were paying.

Families of brides and grooms are not always happy for them to be involved in the financing of the wedding. Marriage is a lifetime partnership with all its own financial responsibilities and this will be something they are only too aware of. They would be unlikely to forbid your financial assistance unless they are absolutely convinced it is the wrong approach, in which case they are most probably right.

Financial contribution to the costs of a wedding by the groom's family is becoming a contemporary issue. Since there is no precedent set for this in wedding traditions, a direct request for money would not be well mannered. If financial help is offered, the case is a little different and needs to be analysed in the light of personal circumstances.

Couples must understand that for many fathers of the bride, meeting the costs of their daughter's wedding is a point of immense personal pride. There is no guarantee that an offer of financial assistance from any front will be well received and every effort must be made to avoid causing offence. In situations where there is an obvious and wide gulf between the finances of the two families, it will be apparent to both and an offer will probably be made tentatively to the groom by his parents for him to sound out with the bride. Financial help is often best tempered with a little euphemism. Instead of talking directly about money, it can be more diplomatic for a groom's family to express a desire to supply the drinks, the flowers or some other expensive item. This certainly runs less risk of embarrassing anyone.

Whilst we are on the subject of financial contribution from third parties, there is a point on which you must be absolutely clear. The moment someone has financial involvement in your wedding, they will probably also expect to be involved in deciding how it should be spent. The more people making a decision, the harder it is to reach and you run the risk of having too many cooks in your kitchen.

Financing a wedding can so easily cause rifts both within and between families and trying to avoid this at all costs, you should want to set a good example. If you find that the divisions between opposing camps start to grow and communication disintegrates, you will need to send in a mediator in the form of your best man, chief bridesmaid, sister, brother or other close relative, but until tempers have cooled, you must stay as firmly out of the picture as possible.

If we are to accept weddings at all in their historical context, we must also accept that for any parent, the wedding of their child is an immense source of pride. To have brought a child up to adult life and to the point at which he or she is ready and able to assume responsibility is quite an achievement. Parents are justified in having personal opinions as to the ways in which their children should be married. The typical wedding tension lies in the fact that part of the process of getting married is a symbolic demonstration of your adult independence from your parents, so the two overlap. If your wedding is to be the happy, memorable occasion it should be, both you and your parents must learn to listen, accept and respect each other's opinions and come to a suitable compromise.

NOTES
1. It is customary for the parents of bridesmaids and other young attendants to pay for their wedding clothing, the style of which is chosen by the bride. Knowledge of this custom cannot be assumed and a bride should be certain of her intentions before inviting children to be bridesmaids. She may want to offer to pay the costs of their clothing from the wedding budget to save the parents the costs. If this is not the case she must make the parents aware that she is expecting them to pay when the invitation is given.

2. It has always, in principle, been customary for the groom to choose and pay for the bride's and bridesmaids' bouquets. This has become increasingly less the case in practice for simple reasons. Most brides will prefer to choose the style and content of their own wedding bouquet themselves. Not only is this an enjoyable task, but in so doing they can ensure it will complement the wedding dress. Furthermore, for practical reasons it has become more usual for the bride's family to organise and pay for all the flowers, both in the church and at the reception venue, and deal only with one florist. The groom does, however, personally or with the help of his best man, organise some gift or bouquet of flowers to present to the two mothers during the reception speeches.

## 6. Budgeting
Having established exactly who is going to pay for it all, you must set yourselves a budget to work towards. Few brides are lucky enough not to have restrictions imposed on the expenditure for their weddings and the only way to overcome this problem is to prioritise the areas you need to consider.

For many brides, the focal point of their imaginings will be the wedding dress. Wedding dresses are such an important part of every culture and it should not really surprise us to find

## Who pays for what? (traditionally)

The following table represents the typical areas of wedding expenditure and whose traditional responsibility it is to pay. Remember to look at the Notes too.

| Cost | Bride's Family | Groom's Family | Note |
|---|---|---|---|
| Wedding dress and veil, shoes etc. | * | | |
| Bridesmaids' clothing | | | 1 |
| Groom's and best man's clothing | | * | |
| Venue/Marquee | * | | |
| Catering and wine | * | | |
| Decorations | * | | |
| Cars for bride etc. | * | | |
| Music/entertainment | * | | |
| Photographs | * | | |
| Invitations | * | | |
| Cake | * | | |
| Ceremony/legal expenses | | * | |
| Ring(s) | | * | |
| Bride's bouquet | | * | 2 |
| Buttonholes | | * | |
| Bouquets for mothers | | * | |
| Bouquets for b/ms | | * | |
| Gifts for b/ms | * | * | |
| Car to church for groom and b/man | | * | |
| Car to reception for B + G | | * | |
| Car to honeymoon | | * | |
| Gift to b/man + ushers | | * | |
| Gift to bride | | * | |
| Gift to groom | * | | |
| Honeymoon expenses | | * | |

G = groom; B = bride; b/ms = bridesmaids; b/man = best man

out how easy it is to spend the cost of an entire wedding on a single dress. Weddings are the only opportunity most of us get to wear such ceremonial dresses and so, naturally, a great deal of thought goes into a bride's appearance on her wedding day.

Money spent on the wedding dress must, however, be in reasonable line with the overall budget. If the dress accounts for more than a small percentage of what you have to spend, you will need to think again. It could come down to a choice of that particular dress or champagne for the speeches.

Beyond her wedding dress, a bride is quite likely to have come to some fairly fixed decisions as to what other areas of the wedding are of personal importance. She may have picked up ideas from magazines or other friends' weddings and while copying someone else's formula is not a wise approach, which we will come to later on, the more weddings you attend and think about, the better feel you do get for what works and why. These areas need to be listed, in priority order, so that focus on what is personally important is not lost. Some brides will consider the flowers to be very important and will be prepared to do without an expensive wedding car in order to be able to afford them. Others will prefer to spend money on an elaborate wedding cake. These are the choices you will make that will help you retain control over the costs of the wedding as well as ensuring that your individuality is stamped firmly on the proceedings.

You will now need to start the long process of asking for quotations from some of the different companies and services you think you might need. Short of employing a professional, there is no way round the fact that this will take you time and attention to detail. The more quotations you get, the better you will be able to judge what a fair price might be and what level of expenditure you can anticipate by following certain different options. When comparing quotations, it is important to be aware of the huge diversity of what is available for weddings and that the quality of the product or service upon which one quotation is based can be infinitely superior or inferior to the next.

Quotations cannot be accurate unless the information on which the price is quoted is as full and detailed as possible. To give yourself the best possible chance of understanding what is available to you, you need to make an extra-special effort to give as much information as possible to companies you are asking to quote. If you have the information to hand when you contact the company involved, you will immediately establish yourself as organised and helpful. This can only do your future relationship good.

Quotations are not always as easy to understand as they might be when they do arrive. Professionals get very used to referring to things by their trade name or in terms of dimensions or quantities. If there is anything included on a quotation that you do not fully understand, it is up to you to ask for an explanation. Remember, too, to look for hidden costs.

## HIDDEN COSTS

Hidden costs are those which you will be likely to incur by accepting the quotation under present scrutiny but which might not come from the same source or indeed be anything to do with the quotation. Perfect examples of these might be marquee costs or catering costs. A marquee company might submit a quotation for a marquee with electric lighting. It is unlikely that this will include the cost or job of getting the electricity to the tent, which depending upon the setting, could mean having to hire a generator or electrician or both. Similarly, menu suggestions sent out by catering companies and hotels in response to wedding enquiries will not always cover the cost of tables and chairs or cutlery, china and glasses, staffing equipment or room charges. These can double the price you would be likely to pay in real terms and thereby make it impossible for you to consider the option. These are things you need to know as soon as possible in order not to waste valuable time. Never be afraid to ask the individual involved to explain any hidden costs they can foresee or for advice on the best methods of overcoming problems. You are not obliged to take their advice, but it could well help.

Very low quotations that are significantly undercutting others need to be mistrusted. They may well be a desperate sales pitch by a company that is close to going out of business and that may not even be around by the time your wedding comes along. If you book them, pay the inevitable deposit and find they are unable to honour their commitment, will you really have the time or the energy to pursue the matter?

Recommendations of companies from friends who may have used them in the past are a good way of finding potential suppliers. You must be aware, however, that a wonderful wedding will be one that is appropriate to your situation, not theirs. The formula that goes to make up a lovely wedding is subject to so many personal factors that what might have worked in one place at one time might never work again. In many ways this is the lovely thing about weddings, that they are so personal.

Dealing with the different companies you are likely to need to put your wedding together will demand a great deal of attention to each area. If you want to be sure of having your favourite flowers in your wedding arrangements and bouquet, you will have to specify what these are, or accept whatever does appear. The less you leave to chance or to uncertainty, the more control you will be able to keep over what actually happens at your wedding. You are well within your rights to ask to see photographs of previous work or letters of commendation from past clients. Once you have chosen your suppliers, you can quite reasonably ask for menu and wine tastings or to see sample flowers. No bona fide professional company would find this approach anything other than natural. As you come to consider the different parts of the wedding, turn to the relevant chapters and sections in this book dealing with each specific part.

If any of this sounds a little negative, take heart! For although you are likely to have many disappointments, you are bound also to be pleasantly surprised by your discoveries. You have the most wonderful opportunity to design your wedding day around all that is most important to you. It is a challenge but one that you should see as enjoyable and worthy of the step which you are taking in life.

# CHAPTER 4
# The Preliminaries

The betrothal stage has always preceded marriage. Betrothal is the old term for engagement and signifies the period of time during which a couple are known to be affianced and plans for the wedding take shape.

The traditional length of the betrothal period varies in history and custom. Since the middle of this century, engagements have become generally shorter. Engagements which fall into the 'average' category are probably no longer than a year and no shorter than six months. To try to put a wedding together in less than six months can be a demanding mission and one that can easily take away all the pleasure to be derived from doing it.

## 1. The ring
The gift of a ring to signify betrothal or marriage is as ancient a custom as marriage itself. Every society and culture in which marriage has been celebrated has had its own symbol of marriage commitment. In Ancient Greece, rings were exchanged by lovers and generally considered to be a precursor to an imminent marriage. Gold was a highly prized possession long before the introduction of coins and in Ancient Egypt, a man would carry his wealth as gold rings worn on the fingers, one of which he would give to his wife, thereby symbolically conferring his worldly goods upon her. In Ancient Rome, not only the lovers, but their parents would exchange rings.

The degree to which the exchange of a ring in betrothal has had a legally binding significance varies, in more recent times giving rise to litigation for breach of contract. Certainly, it has always been considered as a step towards greater and more permanent commitment, particularly if the lovers were forced to be apart through circumstance.

As a symbol of marriage, the ring was sanctified by the Church in the eleventh century and in 1549 was elevated in importance to play a central role in the marriage service itself.

Religions vary according to which finger and on which hand the betrothal and wedding rings should be worn. Sometimes an engagement ring is joined by another during the ceremony, sometimes replaced entirely and sometimes moved from one hand to the other, according to where you are in the world and at what time in history. The left hand has generally been more popular probably for the simple reason that most people are right handed and therefore use their left hand less. So the ring is less likely to get in the way or become damaged. Considering the size of some rings in fashion over the years, this was probably a wise decision. In the seventeenth century popular belief stated that a vein of blood could be traced from the third finger of the left hand right the way to the heart, appropriately named the 'Vena Amoris'.

Rings set with precious and semi-precious stones were first worn only by kings and queens. In ancient times, countless myths and legends grew up surrounding how these stones might have come to be. Sometimes formed from the tears of divine beings, sometimes serpents' eggs, the stories which grew up around gemstones always involved magical happenings and mystical properties. These mystical properties have long been believed to influence the lives of the wearers.

The twelve signs of the Zodiac were originally devised by ancient Babylonian astronomers to represent the twelve phases of what was believed to be the sun's annual rotation of the heavens. It was not until much later that it was understood that the sun was the only thing in the heavens that did not move. This division of twelve still forms the basis of our calendar. Each phase was associated with a particular gemstone, whose power was thought to be stronger during this time. Perhaps to condone a pagan belief that was hard to put down, the Catholic Church also later blessed gemstones with spiritual significance.

The setting of certain gemstones in betrothal and wedding rings according to the birthdates of the wearer has been popular since the Middle Ages, although never quite so much as in Victorian times. In an attempt to combine stones to form phrases of love from the first letter of the name of each stone, some highly questionable fashions for jewellery can still be found today.

Birthstones are still used in engagement rings today, although not as often as before. Their use does not always correspond to the birthdate of the wearer since the choice is often made according to preference for the colour, rather than the meaning.

The following list represents the birthstone according to the month and the star sign with which it is associated and the qualities it is supposed to confer on the wearer.

Capricorn
December 21–January 19 TURQUOISE
Turquoise, from which the word for the colour comes, is a pale greenish-blue opaque stone, sometimes flecked with other colours. It is said to bring harmony, success and happiness.

Aquarius
January 20–February 19 GARNET
Garnet is a dark red stone and is often found close to diamonds. Its colour was associated with blood in Ancient Egypt and was often used in statues of the powerful goddess, Isis. Very fashionable in Victorian times, it was thought to flatter the complexion. The garnet will guard against illness and symbolises fidelity and constancy.

Pisces
February 20–March 20 AMETHYST
Amethyst is a clear stone, the colour of which can vary from a very pale to a very dark purple. It has always been a noble jewel and was once as highly prized as the diamond. It was widely used by the Victorians for mourning jewellery, commemorating the death of loved ones. 'Amethyst' means 'not drunken' and the stone is thought to bring virtue, sobriety and sincerity in all aspects of life.

ARIES
March 21–April 20 AQUAMARINE
Aquamarine varies in colour from the clearest water blue to a
blue-green. It is symbolic of youth, courage and happiness.

TAURUS
April 21–May 20 DIAMOND
The word diamond comes from the Ancient Greek
'Adamas', meaning indomitable and many legends surround
this, the most cherished of all gemstones. Until the fifteenth
century only those of noble birth were allowed to wear
diamonds. Purity and innocence are associated with
diamonds.

GEMINI
May 21–June 20 EMERALD
The green emerald was sacred to the goddess Venus because
its colour was symbolic of fertility and natural growth. Since
she was also the goddess of love, the stone was said to
determine the fidelity of a lover by the quality of its colour.
Emeralds were also thought to have healing properties and
would bring peace to a troubled body or mind. Emeralds are
associated with fidelity and harmony.

CANCER
June 21–July 20 PEARL
Pearls can vary from being tiny irregularly-shaped seed pearls
that resemble grains of rice, to being perfectly round creamy-
white or even black. Pearls have always been the symbol of
purity and wisdom but are not often chosen for engagement
rings probably because of an ancient belief that they were
formed from the tears of mermaids. An alternative stone for
Cancer is agate.

LEO
July 21–August 21 RUBY
Rubies are rich red stones and have always been associated
with wealth. In Hindu, the ruby is called 'Ratnaraj' or king of
precious stones. The Bible says that the price of a virtuous
woman is above that of rubies, but suggests that such women
are hard to find. Rubies worn on the left hand are said to
control desire.

VIRGO
August 22–September 22 PERIDOT
Peridots are usually a yellow shade of green, but can sometimes
be pink and slightly similar to a pale amethyst. They are probably
the least known of all the birthstones, but will bring contentment
and fidelity. Virgos have sometimes also worn sardonyx.

LIBRA
September 23–October 22 SAPPHIRE
Sapphires can be yellow, but more usually range from very pale
to inky-blue. For early Christian scholars their colour represented the blue of heaven and for this reason the sapphire has
been greatly favoured by popes as an aid to repentance. The
sapphire brings peace, wisdom and virtue.

SCORPIO
October 23–November 22 OPAL
Opal is a milky-white stone with flecks of red and green as it
catches the light. For Scorpios it is a symbol of faith and good
fortune and everlasting love. For others it is associated with ill
luck.

SAGITTARIUS
November 23–December 20 TOPAZ
Topaz is a yellow stone, not unlike the yellow citrine and was
thought to be influenced by the moon as it shines most
brightly at night. A topaz will bestow beauty, intelligence and
long life upon its wearer.

If you have decided what sort of engagement ring you would
like, the next question is where is it going to come from? Some
families are fortunate enough to have rings which may have
been engagement rings belonging to relatives and may decide
that these would be suitable gifts to a daughter or daughter-in-
law. Sometimes stones from other rings or pieces of jewellery
will be reset specially for a new bride and to her chosen design.
A really lucky bride will be given the opportunity to commission a jeweller to create her dream ring from stones she will
choose from his stock.
    For most people, however, the choice will be made between
a new or antique ring from retail jewellers or antique shops
and markets.

Retail jewellers sell vast quantities of engagement rings in all sorts of designs and the choice of stone is reasonably large. Because of the mass production, the costs are kept relatively low and they can therefore offer rings to suit all pockets. You would be unlikely to find anything particularly unusual though and for this you would be better off searching in antique jewellery shops and markets.

Second-hand rings are often better value for money than modern alternatives as well as being much more interesting or creative in terms of the way in which stones are set. A word of warning is essential here. If you do buy a second-hand ring, or are given an old family ring that has not been recently repaired, you must have it looked at by a professional jeweller to see that the stones are securely in place before you start wearing it. Jewellery, like everything else, suffers the ravages of time and stones can fall out. Your engagement ring is supposed to last at least your lifetime.

The setting of your chosen stone is as important as the stone itself. Gold, white gold or platinum? – your budget will often make the decision for you. Remember that you will normally continue to wear your engagement ring after you are married and both this and the wedding ring will be worn together. Sometimes brides choose their engagement and wedding rings to match and you should consider this point. Certain shapes of engagement ring can make the wearing of a plain gold band quite difficult. Wedding rings can be set with stones to match those of your engagement ring or be plain bands of gold. Fit is very important and a professional jeweller will be able to size the rings properly for you so that your circulation is not cut off on hot days and the rings do not slip off in the cold. It is also important to consider how the stones should be set in the metal. A claw setting is often considered more elegant, but it can catch on clothing especially stockings and tights. You do not want to have to take your ring off every time you get dressed and nor do you want to risk losing it. Flatter settings can be more practical, so make a point of asking a jeweller to show you the difference.

How much should you spend? Engagement rings are normally paid for by the groom, unless the ring is a family ring. The traditional sum is supposed to be equivalent to one month of his salary. Without being silly about it, you should spend what feels right.

INSURANCE

If your engagement ring is second-hand, you should have it professionally valued and, no matter where it comes from, insured, as you should with any piece of jewellery that you would be sorry to lose. It would be foolish to wear a ring that you could not afford to insure properly. Do remember that an engagement ring is important because of the love it signifies between a couple. It is an expression of deep emotion and commitment and the simplest ring contains the same message as the most elaborate.

Some men feel that it is up to them to choose the engagement ring and in the past, this would often have been the case. Hollywood is probably to blame for the image of a handsome young man on his knees, extracting from his breast pocket a velvet box from which he produces an enormous diamond solitaire. Murmuring words of love, he slips it on the finger of a delighted and beautiful young woman and, miraculously, it is a perfect fit.

Not all men are so easily able to judge the taste and finger size of their ladies, so grooms would be well advised to consult their brides on this issue. A bride should have the chance to help choose the ring she will wear every day for the rest of her life.

## 2. Announcing the engagement

For many couples, the announcement of their engagement will come as a logical development of their relationship over time. For others it may be a surprise or even a shock, particularly if one or other is not in regular contact with their families or if they have only known each other a short time. In the past, the groom would approach the bride's father and formally ask for her hand in marriage before she herself had even been asked and for centuries a favourable paternal reply would usually have been a foregone conclusion. Grooms today often choose to perform this small act of chivalry, more as a mark of respect than anything else and they would be unlikely to do so had they not already popped the question to their future brides.

Whether or not a groom chooses to speak to his fiancée's parents, the families of the couple must be informed of the engagement before all others. If you neglect this, their embarrassment and hurt will be duly justified. Once your families have been told, there is little point in trying to keep an engagement secret.

You will obviously tell your close friends. But what of friends with whom you have·lost touch, or who have moved away? Placing public announcements in the local or national press is the immediate answer. It is a proud and historic moment when you see your names in print. As an incidental point, it has never been considered good manners to congratulate the bride on her marriage, either at the betrothal stage or at the wedding, presumably because it could have undertones of 'Well done, you've managed to get yourself a husband'. One should not worry unduly about this sort of thing any more and this slight lapse in etiquette is unlikely to be intended or received as a deliberate slight.

The cost of placing press announcements is comparatively low. Different newspapers have different forms and each will be helpful to couples if they require information on the form of announcement. Wedding announcements are placed in the 'Court and Social' section of national broadsheets and your engagement will be sitting prettily next to news of what the Royal Family will be doing that day, social appointments of visiting dignitaries and term dates of public schools.

A typical announcement would read:

'Mr J.D. Harris
and Miss F.A. Green

The engagement is announced between John David, eldest son of Mr and Mrs Peter Harris of Minehead, Somerset, and Frances Anne, only daughter of Mr and Mrs Nicholas Green, of Hadley Wood, Hertfordshire.'

The wording of an announcement is more difficult in the case of couples whose parents are divorced, separated, widowed or remarried, so at the end of the chapter are some examples of hypothetical wordings as applicable to particular marital situations.

It is perfectly acceptable to include full addresses on engagement announcements and this helps those friends who might read the announcement to find you and re-establish contact. However, it would also mean that you are likely to receive quantities of promotional literature through the post from companies with an interest in your wedding. Make no mistake, this can be helpful but it can also be intrusive if not desired, so think about this carefully. Even not including your full addresses, you will probably receive some literature, since there are companies who trace full addresses from the sketchiest of information provided in engagement announcements and sell these monthly to the trade.

If and when you decide that you would like to place a formal announcement in any sort of newspaper, it can be done easily and quickly. After telephoning the publication concerned to assess the current cost, the only foolproof method of avoiding spelling mistakes is to write down, or better still, type the announcement exactly as you would like it to appear. You really cannot do it over the telephone. If you have access to a fax machine, so much the better. Some papers will send you a form to fill in, others will leave it very much up to you, but all are extremely helpful. According to how often the paper goes to print, your announcement can appear as little as 24 hours after it is submitted, but you must of course confirm the publication date and let your families know too so they have a chance to buy a copy.

With or without a printed announcement, once your families have been told, you are officially engaged. This does not mean that you must already be sporting a sparkler. It is better to spend time choosing the ring with care than to rush off and buy one in haste, but few women feel really engaged until it is actually on their finger.

Here are some traditional wedding announcements to cover all eventualities.

TRADITIONAL WEDDING ANNOUNCEMENT FORM

Bride = Miss Frances Anne Green
Groom = Mr John David Harris

*Groom's parents divorced or separated but not remarried*

Mr J.D. Harris
Miss F.A. Green
The engagement is announced between John David, eldest son of Mr Peter Harris of Minehead, Somerset and of Mrs Victoria Harris of Petersham, Surrey, and Frances Anne, only daughter of

Mr and Mrs Nicholas Green of Hadley Wood, Hertfordshire.

### Bride's parents divorced or separated but not remarried

Mr J.D. Harris
Miss F.A. Green
The engagement is announced between John David, eldest son of
Mr and Mrs Peter Harris of Minehead, Somerset and Frances
Anne, only daughter of Mr Nicholas Green of Hadley Wood,
Hertfordshire and of Mrs Patricia Green of Ipswich, Suffolk.

### Groom's parents divorced and mother remarried (makes no difference if father remarried, as name doesn't change)

Mr J.D. Harris
Miss F.A. Green
The engagement is announced between John David, eldest son of
Mr Peter Harris of Minehead, Somerset and of Mrs Stephen
Cosby of Cranbrook, Kent, and Frances Anne, only daughter of
Mr and Mrs Nicholas Green of Hadley Wood, Hertfordshire.

### Bride's parents divorced and mother remarried (makes no difference if father remarried, as name doesn't change)

Mr J.D. Harris
Miss F.A. Green
The engagement is announced between John David, eldest son of
Mr and Mrs Peter Harris of Minehead, Somerset, and Frances
Anne, only daughter of Mr Nicholas Green of Hadley Wood,
Hertfordshire, and of Mrs Patrick O'Donnel of Dublin, Eire.

### 1 parent deceased

Mr J.D. Harris
Miss F.A. Green
The engagement is announced between John David, eldest son of
Mr Peter Harris of Minehead, Somerset and the late Mrs Victoria
Harris, and Frances Anne . . .

### Both parents deceased

Mr J.D. Harris

Miss F.A. Green

The engagement is announced between John David, eldest son of the late Mr and Mrs Peter Harris of Minehead, Somerset, and Frances Anne . . .

*Stepfather has brought child up*

Mr J.D. Harris
Miss F.A. Green

The engagement is announced between John David, eldest son of Mrs Stephen Cosby and stepson of Mr Stephen Cosby of Cranbrook, Kent, and Frances Anne . . .

*Stepmother has brought child up*

Mr J.D. Harris
Miss F.A. Green

The engagement is announced between John David, eldest son of Mr Peter Harris and stepson of Mrs Peter Harris of Minehead, Somerset, and Frances Anne . . .

*Bride has previously been married and divorced*

Mr J.D. Harris
Mrs F.A. Peterson

The only change is at the top of the announcement, the rest of the wording remains the same.

*Bride has previously been married and widowed*

Mr J.D. Harris
Mrs F.A. Peterson

The engagement is announced between John David, eldest son of Mr and Mrs Peter Harris, of Minehead, Somerset, and Frances Anne, daughter of Mr and Mrs Nicholas Green, of Hadley Wood, Hertfordshire and widow of the late Mr Geoffrey Peterson.

Titles, such as Dr, The Honourable, Lord, Lady, etc. should naturally be substituted wherever applicable, as should all armed forces ranks. However, if any titles apply to the bride or groom, these are only used at the top or heading of the

announcement. To be absolutely correct, awards and medals
should not be included as these can seem a little pompous.

## 3. Engagement parties

Engagement parties are not an essential part of the business of
getting married. They cost money, can be difficult to organise
and, if too close to the wedding can take time and attention
away from the more important planning. The decision of
whether or not to have one should be made after consideration
of the facts. It is only natural to want to celebrate an
engagement but this happy urge can run away with you,
particularly financially, as you are unlikely as yet to have fully
costed the implications of the forthcoming wedding.

Like weddings, engagement parties come in every conceiv-
able style and size. From an intimate dinner party at home to a
full blown party, with or without food, it is possible for
everyone to mark this important moment in their lives in some
way. If there is to be an engagement party, it is traditional for
the engagement to be formally announced to the assembled
friends and family during the event, perhaps with some very
informal speeches from the couple or their parents. Printed
announcements would then follow. Engagement parties are, on
the whole, fairly short, simple affairs and it is unlikely that you
will be asking anyone to travel a long distance, as they will,
after all, be required to do this for the impending wedding. So
although never ideal, just a drink would do.

The simplest way to plan an engagement party is to arrange
some kind of gathering and this would traditionally take place
at the home of the bride's parents or her own. Few people have
houses large enough to cope with wedding receptions, but
engagement parties, usually smaller and simpler, offer the
perfect opportunity for an intimate gathering in a family
environment. You will have time to think about the party
before plans for the wedding take off. Whether this takes the
form of a meal or a cocktail party is up to you and you should
look for inspiration from the reception ideas suggested in
Section 2. The engagement party should always be kept as
different as possible from intended plans for the wedding so
that neither celebration upstages the other.

# CHAPTER 5
# Picking a Team

A successful wedding is always the result of a team effort. Assuming too much personal responsibility can only lead to chaos. Even superbeings would have problems trying to remember everything that needs to be done, including all the last minute details and it is for precisely this reason that we have the traditional posts of best man and chief bridesmaid.

It is a singular honour to be invited to become such an important member of the wedding team. It shows a degree of intimacy and trust, the result of friendships often built up over a number of years. Honour, however, comes with its own responsibilities. Both the best man and the chief bridesmaid need to be readily available to take over responsibility for certain tasks and should be involved in the wedding plans as early as possible. Quite apart from offering simple practical help to the bride and groom in finding and collecting things for them, making telephone calls and arranging appointments, they may well have good ideas and suggestions of their own, particularly if either has been married and can often take the tension out of family disputes simply by being there. A best man or chief bridesmaid who is not free to help until the day itself, is not going to be able to offer the necessary support which a bride or groom deserves and in many ways it is not fair to ask them to do half a job.

As a result of this statement, any bride or groom might be prompted to rethink the choice they may have already mentally made, in which case it has achieved its purpose.

By far the best way to come to a decision as to who would be the best man or woman for the job is for both of you to sit down and discuss it together, before anyone else is approached or involved. You are making a commitment to spend the rest of your lives together and now is a very good moment to start making joint decisions. It is as important for the bride to support the choice of best man as it is for the groom. Any bride who suspects a certain friend of the groom's of being a little too wild or of encouraging bad behaviour in him is hardly going to feel easy when the stag night arrives. A bride needs to know that the best man will be sensible and loyal to both her and the groom as a couple. They should both like and respect him. He will play an important role in their wedding day and she should be confident that he will play it well, considering himself responsible for their joint welfare.

The best man is usually someone with whom the groom has grown up or with whom he has shared a significant part of his life. A brother or best friend would be an obvious choice. One might assume that he will therefore also know the bride well, but this is not always the case. As people grow up, they can easily lose contact with one another and new friendships are rarely as close. Sometimes the choice of best man will have to be made from the old friends with whom one may have little left in common and the new with whom one has little or no shared history. If a military wedding is to be celebrated with all the pomp and splendour of regimental uniforms, it is appropriate for the groom to pick a best man from his regiment.

There are situations where it is impossible to avoid offending someone by the simple fault of not asking them to be the best man, but if time is taken to explain the problems or reasons as to why the choice was made in this way, this can usually be overcome.

A contemporary issue is the question of a female best man. Although unlikely to become commonplace, there is no hard and fast rule against a groom choosing a female friend or relative in this support role and it is certainly something which is now happening. The best advice would be to suggest that this decision is reached only with the complete agreement of the bride. As a groom you present your best man very much as your best friend and supporter in life and any bride might be forgiven for feeling a little displaced at this honour being bestowed upon another woman.

For both the bride and groom, the presence of a familiar and competent face as the day dawns will be a calming influence.

As you prepare yourselves privately and publicly for your marriage, you will probably spend more time and effort on your appearance than for any other day of your lives. For the bride, if not for the groom as well, the process will take a long time. Just getting dressed is an eternity as you wait as patiently as you can to be laced, buttoned and pinned up. However sweet it is to be surrounded by over-excited underfives, they will do little to encourage your serenity. A bride on the morning of her wedding needs only her chief bridesmaid for company. Intermittent visits from her family will encourage her, but too many people will only make her nerves worse. She may be surprisingly calm, but very little is needed to trigger the trembles.

It is often easier for the bride to make her choice of 'best woman' than the groom's choice of best man. The chief bridesmaid is rarely nowadays called upon to make a speech, although this is by no means unheard of, so her sense of humour and ability for public speaking are not under scrutiny. To call her a chief bridesmaid makes the assumption that she is not and has never yet been married. She can just as easily be a married friend or sister, in which case her proper title would be 'matron of honour'. The terminology is less relevant than the help and support she can offer. A married friend is actually more likely to be able to offer concrete assistance during the wedding plans since she will have been through the process herself and will always understand the bride's emotional and exhaustion levels. It is also flattering to be asked. Few married women, if given the chance, would refuse the opportunity to arrange their weddings again.

The chief bridesmaid must be somebody who enjoys responsibility and is perhaps even a little bossy. If she is from outside the family she will be able to retain a certain amount of detachment, which can be very useful when your mother, sisters and everyone else starts panicking about getting things done or being ready on time. She is in every respect the mirror image of the best man and the same qualities should be sought in both. She will be there to help the bride in all aspects of her appearance and duties, remembering things and picking up the pieces when it is all over. If you, as the bride, can retain a focus of what the wedding day is really all about and leave the practicalities to someone else, you will have fewer sleepless nights and far calmer days. You must feel at ease with your chief bridesmaid and know that she has your best intentions at heart. Competitive friendships are not a good basis for this relationship. Anyone who makes you feel in any way inferior should not be asked.

Dividing up the duties of the team is a purely personal matter. Division is necessary, but it has to be the decision of the bride and groom as to who does what. To list the traditional duties is useful, but do bear in mind that with this, as with any other aspect of your wedding, tradition is a simplifying process and is not intended to make life even more complicated than it already is. The simple fact is that certain goals have to be met and certain things have to be done if the wedding is to take place and it makes sense for these things to be done by those to whom they will represent the least effort. Most wedding traditions come from times when day-to-day life was easier to predict and society was more regimented. Organising a bride's wedding dress and trousseau would have been a simple enough matter for her mother to arrange in the course of her weekly discussions she would have had with her dressmaker.

It is a quite absurd thought that any twentieth-century bride would leave the choice of her honeymoon bikini up to her mother. So be reasonable about what you can expect from yourself as well as others. Do not choose a best man or chief bridesmaid whose time is limited because of a young family, important exams or demanding job as you will only be adding to their problems as well as your own.

There are times when it is impossible to choose your right-hand people, without adding to the demands of their busy lives and it is worth remembering that there is another wedding corps which can be called to command, the ushers.

Ushers traditionally do not assume responsibility until the day of the wedding itself, and because of this, they are usually less involved in the plans for the wedding. Ushers are normally close friends who would be present as guests at your wedding anyway and who spring into action on the day to see that everything is running smoothly at the church in anticipation of your arrival and to seat the guests as they arrive. Their duties are few and easily performed. Have the chief usher responsible for remembering to locate and take possession of the button-holes in good time, which is so often forgotten. A nice way to involve your close friends in your wedding and make them feel a litte more important is to have plenty of ushers. These days, when a bride and groom will have many friends of both sexes in common, there can be no argument against having female as well as male ushers.

Ushers can be called upon to help in other ways. Time is always an important factor at a wedding, particularly when it is running out and having dependable friends who can be relied upon to take responsibility for last-minute details can be very useful. They can be on hand during the reception to give support to the best man in his efforts to ensure that every guest has a drink, or someone to talk to, that every guest has found their place for a seated meal, that older relatives are found chairs quickly and without embarrassment.

Whoever you do decide to involve in the planning of your wedding and however you decide to play it, team meetings are important means of communicating facts and sharing the enjoyment as well as the pressure. Families may be involved in these meetings if the situation is appropriate, but keeping them out might mean you get more done. The chain reaction will mean that the smallest details are the ones on which the largest depend. Getting all those involved together for a drink or over supper will focus their attention and you will certainly feel more confident in your organisation. It can also help to make the whole thing seem more real.

## 1. The best man's duties

Although it should be a personal choice as to exactly which of the many wedding traditions you decide to follow, there are certain things which simply have to be done. Many of the duties the best man would traditionally perform will already have been considered by the bride and groom, and until the day itself dawns, he should try to think of himself as a private secretary, assuming responsibility for the mundane details rather than the executive decisions. He will need to check and recheck that the following things have been done:

- Hiring/cleaning/collecting of morning dress or suits for himself and the groom;
- Ordering of flowers for bride and attendants, buttonholes for himself, groom and immediate families of bride and groom, bouquets/corsages for mothers;
- Arrangement and booking of honeymoon and checking on passports, visas etc.;
- Printing/Collecting of service sheets;
- Nomination of ushers;
- Transport to and from ceremony for all bridal party;
- Accommodation for himself and groom on night before wedding;

- Buying/collecting the ring(s);
- Organisation of stag night;
- Assistance in accommodation of guests, if necessary;
- Assistance with organisation of service i.e. musicians etc.

The wedding day itself is a very different matter and from the very start the best man will be depended on totally. However modern you want to be about it all, there are things which only he can take full responsibility for:-

- Getting the groom to the church ceremony on time;
- Paying church ceremony fees before service on behalf of groom;
- Checking distribution of buttonholes, service sheets;
- Holding ring(s) until needed by minister;
- (Usually) signing the marriage certificate as a witness;
- Assembling bridal party for photographs after ceremony;
- Making sure all guests have transport to reception;
- Escorting bride and groom to their car;
- Escorting bridesmaids to reception;
- Assuming duties of a toast-master if there isn't one i.e.

calling names for receiving line, announcing speeches, speakers and cake-cutting;
- Making sure all guests are given drinks and have people to talk to, that any seating plan has worked;
- Replying to groom's toast to the bridesmaids;
- Reading out telegrams;
- Checking tickets and luggage for honeymoon;
- Making sure bride and groom leave in good time for honeymoon departure;
- Making sure all guests have transport home and/or accommodation.

Even after the wedding certain things need to be considered:

- The best man would certainly be responsible for returning his and the groom's morning dress or suit to hire shop/dry cleaners.
- Either he or the chief bridesmaid would need to be sure to arrange for any wedding presents brought to wedding to be taken home.

## 2. The chief bridesmaid's duties

Throughout the period of planning she should be available to help the bride in any way necessary. Even making telephone calls in search of a specific shade of shoe can be unbelievably time-consuming, and having someone to share the work makes it seem very much easier and a lot more fun. She is a cross between a confidante, a sister and a lady's maid, concerned throughout for the welfare of the bride. If she can see that it is all getting too much, she will be prepared to have a quiet word with the groom and for this reason it is helpful for her to know him quite well. Emotions always run high at weddings and her calm disposition will be admired. If the honeymoon destination is to be kept a secret from the bride, she will need to be told in order to assist in the choice of clothes she takes.

IN ADVANCE

- Helping the bride choose her outfit and those for all bridesmaids and pageboys;
- Organising fittings if necessary;

- Making sure the bride will have all that is needed for the honeymoon, including any injections, visas etc.;
- Helping bride's family keep track of acceptances, presents and chasing up those who are late in replying to invitations;
- Liaising on behalf of bride's family with caterers, florists etc. about last-minute details;
- Organising the hen party.

## ON THE DAY

- Keeping the bride calm;
- Helping her dress;
- Checking contents of honeymoon luggage and that it is sent over to join the groom's;
- Making sure all other bridesmaids are dressed properly;
- Making sure all of bridal party have the right bouquets;
- Smoothing ruffles on arrival at church, holding train if necessary;

- Taking bride's bouquet after procession and returning it following signing of register;
- Assisting bride to change into going-away clothes and last-minute packing for honeymoon.

AFTERWARDS

- Making sure bride's wedding clothes are packed up/returned to parents' house/bride's house/dry cleaners or hire shop;
- Helping with keeping track of presents and thank you letters;
- Ensuring that remaining cake is kept safe.

## 3. The usher's duties

It is normal to have a chief usher who will keep the others informed of their duties. He (or she) will be responsible for ensuring that there is an advance welcoming party at the church for any guests arriving early. With country weddings where the majority of guests are travelling long distances, this is particularly relevant. The chief usher needs to be able to direct guests to the nearest loo or source of refreshment if necessary. He will also need to make certain that the service sheets for the ceremony have been collected and are at the church on time, as well as the buttonholes for the groom, best man and fathers if they do not already have them.

Ushers literally usher guests into their seats. Traditionally, the family and friends of the groom sit on the right-hand side of the aisle, facing the altar and those of the bride on the left. The immediate families of the couple sit in the first pews on these respective sides. It is not a question of importance, rather closeness of relation. Nowadays, the division of friends is less clear as many guests will be shared friends and most contemporary couples favour mixing the friends up on both sides, since it is too silly to have one side of the church crammed with people and the other virtually empty, which can sometimes be the case if attention is not paid to this.

Nothing and no-one can guarantee good weather, but you can and must be prepared for bad. Ushers armed with huge black umbrellas with which to greet arriving guests will always be appreciated in a downpour. Seeking out and collecting these contingency umbrellas is a jolly good duty for a chief usher to concern himself with in the week preceding the wedding.

The chief usher will escort the groom's parents down the aisle to their seats and will do the same for the bride's mother as she arrives just prior to her daughter's entrance. It is rather nice that she should not have to walk down the aisle alone, but the greeting and escorting can equally well be done by a brother or other relative who may or may not be an usher.

Ushers will normally remain towards the back of the church during the wedding ceremony in order to seat any late arrivals. Symbolically, they defend the doors of the church to prevent unwelcome visitors who might try to prevent the marriage and it is easy enough to imagine knights at arms taking over this role in previous centuries. Unlikely though you are to have to call upon the chivalric prowess of your friends, this still means that they will be able to leave the church swiftly after the ceremony and help organise groups for photographs and generally mix with and entertain guests while these are taken.

Once the ceremony is over and the ushers have helped the best man ensure that the bride and groom and the guests are all safely on their way to the reception, their formal duties are more or less completed. As mentioned, ushers can continue to be useful in all sorts of ways depending upon the size of your reception. Getting all your guests to sit down can be quite a task, so posting a few of the friendly faces the guests will already have begun to recognise will get people to their tables quickly and without fuss.

The chief usher will normally attend the wedding rehearsal which will usually take place a day or two before the wedding just to be certain of knowing what needs to be done.

## 4. Toast-masters

The proposal of a 'Toast' has its origins in the seventeenth century. A company of gentlemen drinking together would be asked by one to raise their glasses in appreciation of the beauty (and presumably other bodily delights) of the lady upon whom his interest was currently fixed. The idea was that with her name on the lips of the drinkers, the drink would be spiced up, rather like a piece of spiced toast.

A contemporary toast-master is a master of ceremonies and the presence of a master of ceremonies or guardian of eti- quette is a long tradition at all Royal and formal social events, including weddings. His role is to introduce guests to their hosts, announce meals, speeches and toasts and cake-cutting and generally facilitate the duties and responsibilities of those for whom he is working. He will take the responsibility of keeping a reception to time and liaise with the families on the wedding day. A toast-master does not become involved in wedding plans as such, but will, as far as possible, ensure that the reception runs smoothly on the day. His presence can be an invaluable asset.

If a toast-master is not engaged and it must be said that the great majority of weddings which take place do not use the services of a toast-master, his duties will fall to the best man. Toast-masters traditionally wear a very grand and glorious ceremonial tailcoat with all the trimmings and their presence can greatly add to the colour and ceremony of a wedding, and certainly very formal or large weddings will always benefit from this colourful, professional management.

Ivor Spencer is the Founder and Life President of The Guild of Professional Toast-masters and, having officiated at over 1,000 Royal events, is a worthy spokesman:

Any wedding is a suitable occasion to engage a Toast-master, whether it is to take place at home, in a marquee or in a hotel. Toast-masters can be engaged through The Guild of Professional Toast-masters and all will be fellows of the Guild. There is a great deal of difference between the way in which a professional Toast-master will carry out his duties and one who is not professional. Keeping control over what is happening in a low-key fashion takes experience and the demands made upon a Toast-master vary according to the situation in which he finds himself. Adaptability is an important quality.

As President of The Guild of Professional Toast-masters, I often receive letters from irate hosts who have mistakenly engaged Toast-masters claiming to be members of professional organisations, but who in fact are not. On one occasion a cowboy Toast-master actually told some blue jokes. Anyone other than a professional Toast-master can ruin the occasion and however low his fee might have been, it will have been too high.

# SECTION TWO

# Planning the Reception

# Introductory Advice

Wedding receptions can take a great deal more planning than the religious or civil ceremonies they follow. To many brides it would certainly seem logical to concentrate initially upon plans for the ceremony which is, after all, the single most significant part of a wedding.

Wedding logic is not, however, the most straightforward and while you should not be discouraged from contacting the religious minister or Registrar you hope will marry you, marriage ceremonies should not be confirmed before all the investigative work has been undertaken for the reception.

The purpose of this statement is to ensure that you do not find yourself in the increasingly common situation of a bride committed to a ceremony or service at a certain time and date who has not already booked an appropriate reception venue and type. In certain areas, the number of places in which wedding receptions are held may not be very great and the individual tastes of a bride may narrow this choice down even further. It is quite likely that there is no shortage of churches of various denominations within the same area and the greater number of weddings which take place will converge on this smaller number of venues. Not surprisingly, families will place confirmed bookings for wedding receptions well in advance in order to ensure the availability of their first choice of venue, date and time. This may not leave a wide number of dates free for a bride who has not acted swiftly and she may find herself very restricted in her choice if she is still determined to hold her wedding reception in one of a limited number of venues.

Recent changes to the law now allow certain types of venues to apply for licences to hold civil marriage ceremonies. The implications of these changes have widened the scope of opportunity immensely for couples who previously would have had to have been married in one or other of their local Register offices. The implications of these changes are dealt with later but it is important to realise that while a wedding ceremony and reception held in one venue might simplify the arrangements, these latest developments will only have added to the appeal of specific venues for weddings and will not make them easier to book.

While seldom as urgent as the problem of location, other factors involved in the wedding reception could be classed within this same category, i.e. needing prompt action. Popular wedding photographers, toast-masters, florists and caterers, cake-makers and car hire companies, dressmakers and marquee companies also get booked up for weddings well in advance. To work out your personal best wedding formula, you need to allow plenty of time for sourcing, comparing and deciding what will work for you. When the greater number of your chosen suppliers can match with your chosen venue AND the church, synagogue or register office in which you are to be married can accommodate the wedding, THEN you are in a position to confirm a particular date. Any other sequence of events is risky and could lead to much disappointment on your part as well as a great deal more work.

# CHAPTER 1
# What Type of Reception?

Before you answer this question, try to clear your mind of all the ideas you will naturally have picked up from friends' weddings or from reading magazines or books. Being too set in your mind at this stage can easily mean you stubbornly pursue an option while all the time a different, far more suitable one is staring you in the face but, by the time you see sense, it is often too late to change the plans. You cannot depend on a particular scenario just because it worked for somebody else. You have to find your own formula and should always start with a clean sheet.

## NUMBERS

Any budget you have already decided on, or are yet to set in the light of the quotations which you will probably already have started to request, will have to be divided between the number of guests invited to your wedding, so breaking down a budget depends upon having a reliable number of guests worked out, based upon a list.

Since the bride's family has for so long traditionally met the costs of a wedding, the final say in numbers has usually been left up to them, budget and space permitting. Until you know how many guests you will be likely to have, it is very difficult to anticipate the size of venue or marquee needed and the cost implications of various different types of reception. Compile a basic list with the help of both families and you will be off to a good start.

## SETTING

If you are lucky enough to be able to consider holding your wedding reception at home, you should certainly investigate this option fully before others. Not only is it appropriate for a family wedding reception to be held at home and likely to be a far more personal and intimate event as a result, but this will help you retain greater control over the costs. Contrary to popular belief, marquees do not have to be expensive. Choosing the right sort of marquee and using it correctly can offer many more brides the option of having their wedding receptions at home. Hiring a

marquee is really a complicated business, so if you are thinking
of doing so, it would be wise to read the chapter covering
marquees before coming to any firm conclusions.

If you cannot consider a wedding reception held at home,
you will need to look further afield. Hotels and special
reception venues within an area tend to be well known, but
there are plenty of alternatives, which are discussed later.

## TIME OF YEAR

For some couples, the season in which they are married will be
determined by outside factors, such as postings overseas, new
jobs, exams or other commitments, rather than making the
choice because they would particularly like a summer or winter
wedding.

Although in general weddings are becoming less seasonal,
the summer months are still the most popular, say from the
beginning of June to the end of September. It is certainly
easier to plan a summer wedding in some ways – the days are
warmer and longer, popular flowers are in season and therefore affordable. There is also a historical tradition of summer
weddings for a number of very natural reasons. Marriages have
always involved feasting. This can only be possible when food
is plentiful and food for celebrations has always been somehow
special and not normally available. Marriages in the summer
months would lead to the birth of children the following
spring, when warmer weather and greater food availability
would make it easier to nurse newborn babies.

Being no longer dependent upon the seasons for food, we can
use the changes provided by the passage of each year to our
advantage, particularly in the dramatic interpretation of a wedding. The Summer Wedding is the Midsummer feast which
looks to and welcomes nature with all its sunny green light and
newness of life. The Winter Wedding is the challenge to sleeping
creation, drawing itself into warmth and creating points of light
in the quiet darkness of long nights. These highly symbolic
interpretations give ample opportunity for creativity.

## TIMING

However daunting the wedding might seem at times in anticipation, most newly-married women will tell you, their eyes
mistily distant, just how quickly the day seemed to fly past. All
too soon you go from being Mr and Mrs really important to

Mr and Mrs really rather ordinary like everyone else.

Weddings which start late in the day compress the time a bride spends being the bride into a far shorter period than those which make better use of the 24 hours. Because of nerves of excitement, it can be far harder to enjoy the hours before the wedding takes place than the hours of celebration which follow the marriage. By choosing to marry at a later time in the day, be sure that you are not denying yourself the opportunity to enjoy the whole experience. Plan the hours before a late ceremony carefully so that you are not simply waiting around to get going.

A traditional wedding reception does take several hours. A reception at which the majority of guests are expected to stand should not be allowed to become drawn out and exhausting for those without chairs. One of the most common complaints made about other people's weddings is the length of time we were expected to stand around – while photographs are taken or during the reception itself. Physical discomfort does lead to

---

TIMING ALLOWANCES

*Ceremony* – Church – Anglican/Scottish/R.C. without mass
   approximately 30–45 minutes
   – Synagogue approximately 30–45 minutes
   – Register Office/Civil Ceremony approximately
   20–30 minutes
   – R.C. with nuptial mass 1hr 15 mins

---

SAMPLE TIMINGS FOR A TRADITIONAL WEDDING

| | |
|---|---|
| 14.00 | Service |
| 14.45 | Photographs |
| 15.00 | Leave for reception venue |
| 15.15–16.45 | Reception |
| 16.45–17.15 | Speeches |
| 17.30 | Cake cut |
| 18.00–18.30 | Bride and groom leave |

This is relatively short in essence, but still manages to cover a minimum period of four hours. If a full meal is to take place after the reception period, you will need to allow at least an extra hour and a half to the timings.

exhaustion and it is difficult to enjoy yourself when you are tired. Stand up receptions mean short receptions and the maximum availability of seating nonetheless for those who cannot be realistically expected to stand for more than a few minutes, be they young, old or even pregnant.

## Photographs

Dealing with photographers and preventing lengthy delays is covered later on, but never plan to spend more than 15 minutes having photographs immediately after the ceremony.

## Receiving lines

These are the best way to make sure that all guests are greeted and welcomed on arrival at the reception and introduced to important members of both families. It is hard to process the line at a faster pace than 30 to 60 seconds per guest. If you expect up to a hundred guests, allow an hour for the receiving line during which drinks should be served to all the guests, whether or not they have already been received. 150–200 guests will usually take the best part of an hour and a half.

## Reception

To be strictly correct, the time during which your guests are received by the families and served drinks constitutes the reception regardless of whether or not more substantial provisions are planned to follow. In France this is known as a Vin D'Honneur, to which all guests from the ceremony will be invited for a length of time prescribed on the invitations which will have been sent. A more intimate family dinner or luncheon may well follow the Vin D'Honneur after which those not invited to stay will depart with no ill feelings. This is an accepted tradition in France and helps to keep wedding costs down for French brides. Unfortunately there is no comparable tradition in this country and all guests attending the ceremony must be invited to whatever is planned to follow or you risk giving offence.

Receptions, whether followed by a meal or straight away by speeches should not be allowed to go on for more than an hour and a half or at the very upper limit, two hours.

*Meals*
Timing allowances for meals do obviously depend upon the
number of courses and the way in which the food is to be
served and eaten.

Guests following a seating plan usually take at least ten
minutes to settle themselves in their places. Each course served
should be allocated 20–30 minutes with a brief interlude of
five minutes or so in between.

*Speeches*
Well-planned and well-rehearsed amusing and eloquent wedding
speeches are a joyful, entertaining part of a wedding. Badly
constructed speeches delivered without enjoyment can be excru-
ciatingly embarrassing. Logic must prevail in the length of time
any one speechgiver plans to monopolise the attention of the
guests. Nobody should plan to speak for more than about 15
minutes for risk of boring the guests. In general, three wedding
speeches will require about half an hour. Be sure to find out how
long the speakers intend to take and let your caterer know.

WEDDING CAKE
The wedding cake should be cut after the speeches and toasts
are finished and never before. Hotel and catering staff often
encourage couples to cut the cake before the speeches take
place so that they are able to remove it, cut it up and bring it
back to serve with coffee as soon as the speeches are over.
While we must have some sympathy for the reasons behind
this encouragement, the practice is frankly wrong.

Apart from the vows the bride and groom will make, the
cutting of the cake is the single most important symbolic
moment at a wedding. The wedding cake is the legacy of
centuries of belief in the power of symbols of fertility. If you
cut the cake before the speeches you risk a large number of
guests missing the moment. The speeches help to focus the
minds of the guests back to the issue at hand, which is your
marriage, and build up to the climax of the reception when the
cake is finally cut.

DEPARTURE
We have already mentioned the point of etiquette that states
that wedding guests do not leave before the bride and groom.
In the past it was normal for couples to leave their receptions

promptly, the guests continuing the celebrations after they had gone. The assumption was that the couple would not have had the chance to spend much time together and certainly would not have had an intimate knowledge of each other and that they would long for the privacy of their newly-married status.

Nowadays it is far more usual for the bride and groom to wish to stay on for whatever continuation is planned and this does cause a problem for those guests who need to leave the reception. Think again about what implications this might have on your anticipated plans.

### EVENING PARTIES

Evening parties, following afternoon wedding receptions are very popular. They give the bride and groom the chance to enjoy the more relaxed part of the wedding day with their family and friends, once all the formality and responsibility are over.

There are two types of evening party. The first of these is a natural continuation of the preceding events of the day, with no formal break in between and the same guests in attendance. The second is a separate event entirely, for which separate invitations have been sent and to which different, or additional guests have been invited. Guests arriving at an evening party should never be made to feel that they are coming in to the tail end of something. Tables should be newly laid, ashtrays cleaned, bars reset and the families on hand to greet them.

### APPROPRIATENESS

Once again we return to this important topic. Weddings must be planned in the context of life in general and in accordance with social and financial positions. This is not, it must be stressed, a question of class.

Social confidence comes from experience. Families or individuals who do not have much experience in organising parties or in entertaining in general would be most unwise to set themselves goals for a wedding that are too demanding or difficult to achieve. They are much better off keeping things simple and straightforward

### HOW BIG IS A GUEST?

Roughly speaking, a standing guest will require 10 square feet of space and a seated guest will require anything up to double this amount. To find the square footage of a room or marquee, you need to multiply the length of the room or marquee by its breadth. For example, a marquee measuring 60' × 40' will give a square footage of 2,400 square feet and will accommodate 240 guests standing, and up to 120 guests seated at round tables. Naturally, the size of the tables and the amount of space left in between them do make a difference. This marquee would be generous in terms of space and allow room for a dance floor/area on which guests can stand and have drinks before sitting down to eat.

Depending on their size, hotels, marquees and other reception venues will have a maximum number of guests who can be realistically accommodated according to various different room layouts and different styles of reception.

Finding out that you have too many guests for the venue once the invitations have gone out and replies been received could well mean either having to change the style of the reception at the last minute or somehow find a way to reduce the number of guests. Public licensed venues have legal limits of guests they are allowed to accommodate and they should not be asked to break these regulations, even if they were prepared to. They are for the sake of fire safety, which should concern us all.

Avoid finding yourself in this situation by keeping firm control over the number of guests invited to the wedding from the start. The positive versus negative reply ratio is about 60/40 or 70/30 depending upon how soon or late you send your invitations and the warning period you have thereby given. Nothing, however, can guarantee the number of refusals or acceptances you can expect. Provided you do not leave it dreadfully late, there is no reason why invitations may not be sent in batches, taking stock of replies and calculating how many guests you are accumulating as time goes on.

## Dietary and Religious Requirements

Vegetarianism, veganism and religious laws governing foods are matters of conscience to those who practise these dietary regimes. If you invite someone to your wedding it is because you want them to enjoy the day, so considering what certain guests might need is to be added to your agenda of discussion with your hotel or caterer.

You will be expected to warn any caterer in advance of vegetarian alternatives you would like them to provide for your guests and what percentage of the guests this involves. The only way you can possibly know this is by making an effort to find out. When you send your invitations, include a little slip of paper saying 'If you have any special dietary requirements, please fill in and return', with space for names and type of food required. Even if you are not planning a full meal, this will still help your caterer to ensure that whatever food is planned will be enjoyed.

## DOING IT YOURSELF

It is possible, given the presence of a large, helpful and talented family, to cater for and decorate your own wedding reception and this will certainly help you to save money.

To what degree the bride and groom are actually involved in the physical preparations must be a matter for personal consideration, but they must be aware of the pressure they will already be under and understand that they may not be able to take all that much responsibility for things themselves.

Anyone involved in actually putting together any area of the wedding, be it flowers, cake-making, dressmaking, catering, must have had previous experience on which to draw. None of these things are as easy as talented individuals can make them look. Consider this fact very seriously before allowing anyone to take over an area of your wedding, however good their intentions are.

## INSURANCE

As soon as you have established the likely level of wedding expenditure you must consider insurance. If for any reason the wedding had to be postponed, it can be very hard to find the money again, particularly bearing in mind that even if the wedding is cancelled well in advance of the date, you are quite likely to have already paid out a substantial sum in deposits. If the reception is to be held at home, either yours or someone else's, it is worth contacting the company which deals with the ordinary household and contents cover to see whether they are prepared to cover the wedding costs for a small extra premium. As an alternative, you might contact one of the larger insurance firms directly to see whether they have, as many do, a special wedding insurance package. Just make sure that the amount of cover provided by the premium is in line with what you are planning to spend.

### DRINKS

The traditional celebratory drink is champagne. Champagne is a sparkling wine produced in the Champagne region of France and only wine produced in this area may be called champagne. This is not to say that other areas of France and indeed, other countries, do not produce excellent sparkling wines of comparable quality. 'Méthode Champenoise' refers to such wines, which use the same grape and the same techniques. The exclusivity of the term champagne accounts for the fact that it is often staggeringly more expensive than others of similar quality.

Given the choice, most families would prefer to serve champagne at weddings, but the high cost involved can make this impossible. If you consider that during the average wedding reception a single guest might well get through the best part of a bottle the cost will add up.

Wines are normally sold in bottles of 75cl, being three-quarters of a litre. This size of bottle gives exactly six glasses. To calculate wine allowances, the following guidelines will help. These allowances are *generous*. Most caterers and hotels will charge for what is drunk, 'sale or return', so in this case you can safely overorder a little to ensure the wine does not run out.

---

### DRINK ALLOWANCES PER GUEST

| | |
|---|---|
| Champagne/sparkling wine on arrival for | |
| 1.5–2 hours | 3/4 glasses |
| Champagne throughout for 4 hours | 5/6 glasses |
| Champagne for speeches and toasts only | 1/2 glasses |
| | |
| White wine with starter | 1/2 glasses |
| White/red wine with main course | 3/4 glasses |
| Wine/champagne with pudding | 1/2 glasses |

Liqueurs/port/brandy – less than half your guests will be likely to accept one of these.

---

*Soft drinks and water*
During the course of a wedding reception, most guests will
have at least one soft drink, whether they are also drinking
alcohol or not. If you are serving a meal, you must supply
water. Allow half a litre of water per person and half a litre of
soft drinks. If the weather is very hot, or dancing involved, you
may need to double this quantity.

*Beers*
Serving beer at evening parties is quite common practice and
what proportion of your guests is likely to drink beer is best
left up to you to judge. Beer in quantity is most economically
bought in kegs, which usually give about 80 pints each. Local
beers or ales should always be chosen, for local interest and the
sake of economy.

*Creative alternatives*
Champagne is not always everyone's first choice. Pimm's
works well for a summer wedding and has the advantage that it
can be made strong or weak, so you can control the intoxica-
tion of your guests! Try serving it ready mixed in jugs stuffed
full of fresh mint and sliced fruits with plenty of cucumber,
lemon juice and ice. Few drinks are more delicious and
refreshing in hot weather.
   Sparkling wine served in place of champagne can be spiced
up a little by the addition of a dash of fruit liqueur. Cassis is
the most well known, but try Crème de Mûre, which makes
the drink a beautiful smokey grey/purple and flavours it with
blackberries, as opposed to blackcurrants. Eaux de vie are
clear fruit liqueurs, so do not colour the drink, but are equally
good for flavour. Framboise is popular and so are pear and
peach. In place of liqueurs, you might like to try peach nectar
with sparkling wine, which makes a Bellini, or pear juice as
alternatives to Buck's Fizz. You can always add a slice or berry
of the fruit in question too. Blue Curação mixed with champagne is refreshing and makes an unusually coloured drink.
Because of the sweetness of fruit liqueurs and juices, only very
dry sparkling wine should be used. Many of these fruit nectars
and liqueurs are commonly available in larger supermarkets so
you should have no trouble finding them to try out any of
these suggestions. Liqueurs mixed with wines should be used
sparingly, say one bottle to twenty-five drinks.

Like Pimm's, fruit punches, alcoholic or not, are very refreshing for summer. In winter a glass of mulled wine can help guests feel seasonal and welcome on arrival from the cold. Mulled cider is another less well-known option that follows the same principle and for its richness and icebreaking qualities, a hot butter rum punch is hard to beat.

English country wines are becoming more readily available and some are very good indeed. There can be nothing more appropriate for an English country wedding.

Always spare a thought for the drivers and plan a nice choice of soft drinks. Orange juice and water are not the only options. Non-alcoholic fruit punches made with freshly squeezed juices are far nicer and much more interesting. Don't forget that one can buy perfectly good quality non-alcoholic or low-alcohol wines and beers.

### GLORIOUS FOOD

Wedding receptions are best categorised by the type of food served and the way in which it is served. Food is wonderful stuff. It can be crisp and fresh and wholesome, it can be delicate or intellectual, it can be the ultimate in decadence and self indulgence and it can be themed and amusing. It can also be dry, boring and unappetising. As a nation, we are not known for our food. Rather than looking for something a little different and exciting, we all too often choose fairly safe options.

A wedding is not an appropriate occasion to choose as a method of introducing your friends and relatives to extraordinary foods that they are unlikely to either like or eat. However, just because you accept this fact you do not have to be boring about what you do serve. Wedding buffets do not always have to be composed of coronation chicken and dressed salmon. After several in one season, your guests may very well begin to question the appeal of creamy curried chicken and cold fish. Stylish compromises can be found between catering for the plainer taste and offering food that has a certain flair.

Brides and grooms and their families should be encouraged to spend longer in consideration of the menu than is normally the case. Many assumptions made, that food must be hot or it must be cold or that it must be highly decorated, are not necessarily the case at all and do nothing to encourage chefs to use a little more creativity in drawing up suggested menus.

# CHAPTER 2
# The Sit Down Meal

The only way in which it is possible to do justice to food that has been prepared with thought and care, is to sit at a table, in comfort, with a knife and a fork. The importance of meals shared with family and friends is emphasised in many religions.

A seated meal can be served hot or cold. Cold food should only really be served at summer weddings. A 'hot sit down meal' will mean at least one course will be hot, usually the main course and this will need both preparation space and sufficient cooking equipment on site, both of which may need to be hired and if so, they come into the category of hidden costs.

Many people assume that a seated, served meal is in some way particularly formal. Sitting at a table to eat is something most of us do every day, so where is the formality? Asking friends round for an informal supper does not mean that you will stand up to eat or sit on the floor rather than at the table. The tradition we have somehow allowed to develop in this country of expecting guests to stand up to eat a meal, or balance precariously on the edge of a piece of furniture does not allow for the undisturbed appreciation of culinary talent and would certainly never be tolerated in countries where food is given worthier respect.

Waiting staff form the link between the preparation of the food and the guests who will eat it. They are an essential and far too seldom respected part of the team which can make your wedding reception everything it should be. More than anything else, it is the way in which food is served by the staff, their manner, appearance and performance of their duties that will decide whether or not your wedding reception has a note of formality or informality.

SILVER SERVICE
This is the term used to describe the serving of food by waiters or waitresses, using a serving spoon and fork together in one hand to transfer food from a platter to the plate of each guest

at the table. Food is always served from the left and finished plates cleared from and wine served to the right of each guest. Hot main courses are almost always served in this manner, for obvious reasons while starters and puddings may already be on the plate when they arrive and this is known as plated.

BUTLER SERVICE
This is a more intimate, informal service of food involving the waiter or waitress (but of course in times past, the butler), bringing a platter of food to each guest in turn who then serves him or herself. This method is not appropriate for large wedding receptions as guests are never as speedy or adept with a spoon and fork as a professional.

# CHAPTER 3
# Buffets

'Buffet' refers to any style of food that is served from a central point rather than at individual tables and can of course mean that the guests then do sit at tables, with or without a seating plan. Perhaps more commonly, buffets are chosen when space or budget do not permit tables for all the guests and involve what is termed 'fork' food, i.e. food that is to be eaten by the majority of guests, standing up.

Depending upon which of the above scenarios is intended, different guidelines need to apply.

## 1. Seated buffets

A seated buffet is a good compromise between the comfort and organisation of tables and chairs and the informality or perhaps variety of being able to choose what to eat.

Buffets have to be well planned and well operated. Most caterers will understand that the most efficient buffet is double-ended so that two sets of guests can be served at one go. This involves plates placed at both ends and a selection of dishes mirrored towards the middle of the table.

Guests at a seated buffet should first be invited to sit down, whether or not a starter is planned to be taken to the table before they are expected to then stand to take their food from the buffet table. Starting with the top table, each table of guests should then be invited to approach the buffet individually so that a long queue does not develop and the staff have time to replenish the dishes and bowls as they empty. Buffet menus are rarely cheaper in essence than menus for served meals since a good caterer will be concerned to provide enough of each option for everyone present to have some. This inevitably leads to an overproduction of food to cover all eventualities. You really can tell how good a caterer is by what is left for the last table of guests. Food should not run out. All buffets should be served by members of staff. This is not to counteract greed on the part of your guests, but to ensure that the food still looks attractive and appetising when it is on the plate of each guest, rather than ending up in an ugly pile.

## 2. Stand up buffets
It is truly difficult to balance a plate, a glass and cutlery between mouthfuls if only because we are trying so hard not to drop food on our clothes.

Whatever our personal views on being expected to stand up and eat, there are certain situations where there is little choice. If space or budget is truly limited and tables and chairs cannot be provided elsewhere and the idea of substantial canapés as a replacement does not appeal, it can be done. The following criteria MUST however apply:

- Small tables of some description are placed around the room so that guests can at least put their glasses, bags, hats etc. down while eating.

- Enough staff are provided to clear plates away as they are finished and make sure the room does not end up looking like a kitchen.

- Food is served in fork-sized pieces. It is impossible not to wipe salad dressing all over your face if you have to pick up an entire lettuce leaf with just a fork. You cannot cut food if you are standing up.

● Meat and fish must be filleted and off the bone. Nothing which might have to come out again should have to go in the mouth in the first place.

● No runny sauces or salad dressings should be served. The same applies to cream for puddings. Caterers will often use single pouring cream rather than whipped or double and unfortunately, gravity is not always kind. Ask them to whip the cream before serving it.

● Certain things are just impossible to pick up delicately with a fork – cherry tomatoes, for example.

## 3. Table buffets

This is a rather modern invention and works well at summer weddings where all guests have tables to sit at and an informal service is required. Rather than stand in queues for food, guests are brought their table's allocation of dishes in bowls or on platters by the staff. Having placed the food on the tables, the staff leave the guests to pass the food round and serve themselves, rather as you would at home. Because guests have to talk to and help each other, the ice is immediately broken and the inevitable result is that someone at each table takes charge of passing round and helping others. Guests are then free to have seconds at their leisure and finally, the staff collect the empty bowls and platters with the finished plates.

This style of service should only be chosen if all the food is intended to be served cold. Depending upon the number of dishes planned for each table, thought must be given to leaving enough space in the centre of each table and this may mean reducing the number of guests at each table.

## 4. Buffet variations

According to choice, buffets can require more space and involve so much additional work on the part of both staff and guests that the only real advantage they have over other forms of food service is the variety of tempting dishes on offer. As such, they are a wonderful opportunity to indulge your tastes and look for ways to be creative with the food.

Buffets can be highly stylised, seasonal, hot or cold or both. They can also take the form of a barbecue which would be especially appropriate for an evening party or very informal reception. Barbecue food can be every bit as creative and exciting as other types of food. Remember too, that not every course necessarily has to be served in the same way. A plated starter for every guest could be followed by a table buffet main course and finished off by a superb Mrs Beeton style pudding selection placed on a table in the middle of the marquee or room and lit for effect. Variety can be the spice of life in all ways and surprising your guests in a gentle, acceptable manner will keep their interest in what is to come next. Always involve your caterer and seek suggestions and advice. You never know what might come of it.

One outside catering company with a reputation for creative choice and presentation of buffets is Cottage Caterers. Here they offer inspiration on the subject of buffets.

# BUFFETS

A Buffet is the show piece for the food at your wedding.
It should be magnificent to look at and, of course, delicious to eat.

The Buffet is all about presentation. Raised platforms and tiered stands can be used to create different heights across the table, allowing the food to be displayed at varying levels. The Buffet table itself can be dressed with fresh fruit and flowers – a single, large centre piece can be very impressive, or tiny trails of ivy and honeysuckle can be intertwined amongst the platters of food. The food itself should be attractively presented and displayed on a variety of dishes and plates. Coloured glass dishes are currently very fashionable and make stunning back-drops for cold salads and fish. Large flat baskets, marble 'lazy-Susans' and unusually shaped glass bowls can also help to contribute to the overall impression.

It is also important to remember that the Buffet table needs to be set up with at least two serving points, to ensure that guests are not kept waiting in line for too long.

It is often popular to offer a starter course before the main Buffet. This can either take the form of a 'walking starter' or the more traditional plated starter. With the combination of people travelling over long distances to attend the wedding and the afternoon timing of the church service, the guests are frequently very hungry once they arrive at the reception. The walking starter is an ideal way of offering slightly more substantial food whilst the receiving line is underway. We like to suggest that a selection of six different canapés per person are chosen and these are handed around for the hour or so before the main dinner.

Alternatively, a selection of two or three delicate canapés can be offered with pre-dinner drinks, before a light starter. The starter should be arranged on individual plates and decorated with twists of fresh fruit or sprigs of herbs. It can then be placed on the tables, before the guests have sat down and then warm brown and white bread rolls can be served from large baskets.

Vegetarians should not be forgotten when planning a Buffet Meal. All too often the vegetarians are left to fill their plates with salads and little else. Savoury cheesecakes, colourful terrines or rich pastry tarts are often very popular – with both vegetarians and non-vegetarians. Beware not to limit your quantities too much!

# Notes on Planning a Summer Buffet

It is easy to overdo the selection of food offered at a summer buffet. People tend to take a spoonful of all the dishes on offer and they end up with a mountain of food jumbled together on one plate. We have found that a maximum of four 'meat' dishes and three salads (one green, leafy salad, one mayonnaise dressed salad and one colourful salad) ensures the right balance – the buffet table brims with an abundance of food and once on the plate, the guest can look forward to a delicious dinner.

Following on from the main course, the desserts should be lavish – mouthwatering chocolate soufflés, meltingly rich meringues with cream and exotic fruit salads. These can be displayed and served from the buffet table or can be taken to the guests and silver served.

An increasingly popular way of serving the cheeseboard is to set it out on the buffet table following the meal. This way people can come back to it for a nibble throughout the course of the evening. A selection of cheeses (including a whole Brie, a blue cheese, a soft cheese and a Cheddar truckle) can look spectacular arranged with fresh fruit, biscuits and celery.

# A TRADITIONAL SUMMER BUFFET

A selection of three light canapés

\* \* \*

STARTER

Fanned Segments of Pink Grapefruit with Balls of Elderflower Sorbet
decorated with a Sprig of Mint

\* \* \*

MAIN COURSE

Fresh Tuna seared with Lime and Ginger
Cold Fillet of Beef with a Béarnaise Sauce
Smoked Chicken, Almond and Watercress Platter
Courgette Timbale with a Tomato Coulis, sprinkled with Toasted
Breadcrumbs

\* \* \*

Minted Hot New Potatoes
Sun dried Tomato, Mango and Basil Salad
Cucumber, Dill and Yoghurt Salad
Leafy Green Salad with a Mustard and Honey Dressing

\* \* \*

DESSERT

A Ring of French Vanilla Ice-Cream filled with Fresh Summer
Berries
Sunken Chocolate Soufflé with Black Cherries and Cream
Passion Fruit Mousse with a Fresh Mango Coulis

\* \* \*

Coffee and Chocolate Dipped Fruit

\* \* \*

CHEESEBOARD

To be arranged on the buffet table and left for the guests
to help themselves.
Cheeseboard to include a selection of cheeses, biscuits, celery and fruit.

# Notes on Planning a Winter Buffet

Again the selection of dishes on offer should not overwhelm the guests –
three main course dishes ensure a good selection. The most important
part of a hot buffet is guaranteeing that the food is piping hot when it is
served and is still piping hot by the time the guests get back to their
tables. Old fashioned colonial style chafing dishes look wonderful and are
very efficient at keeping the food hot, and plates straight out of the hot
cupboard ensure nothing cools down too quickly! Disposable plate
holders stop the guests burning their hands.

## A WARMING WINTER HOT BUFFET

A selection of three hot canapés

* * *

### STARTER

Warmed Wild Mushroom Tartlets with a Watercress Sauce
Assorted Hot Bread Rolls and Butter

* * *

### MAIN COURSE

Apricot Stuffed Crowned Roast
King Prawn Provençale, decorated with Whole Prawns and Slices of Lemon
Raised Game Pie with a Rich Cranberry Gravy

* * *

Pommes Lyonnaise
Roasted Winter Vegetables

* * *

### DESSERT

Crème Brûlée with Spiced Cherries
Old Fashioned Steamed Chocolate Pudding with a Hot Chocolate Sauce
Hot Peaches in Cinnamon

* * *

### CHEESE COURSE

Baskets of Hot Cheese Savouries including Welsh Rarebit,
Gruyère Puffs and Roquefort Tartlets

* * *

Coffee and Home-made Truffles

# Notes on Planning an Alternative Buffet

With outside catering becoming more sophisticated and clients becoming more adventurous, caterers are increasingly asked to come up with new ideas for buffets. One theme which has been very popular recently is our Chinese style buffet. Instead of a buffet table, individual food carts with stripy canopies are set up around the room. The chefs then stir fry the food in front of the guests and serve it straight from the wok. The theme can then be carried through to the overall decoration of the marquee – Chinese lanterns, dragons, red silk tablecloths, chopsticks etc.

## A CHINESE STYLE BUFFET

A selection of three Oriental canapés to include:
Assorted Wontons and Dim Sum with a Plum Sauce
Prawn, Sesame Seed and Spring Onion Croutons
Chinese Water Chestnut and Bacon Rolls

★   ★   ★

ON THE TABLES

Baskets of Deep Fried Seaweed
Prawn Crackers
Chicken and Pork Satays with Peanut Sauce

★   ★   ★

MAIN COURSE

King Prawns with Green Peppers and Garlic
Beef Teriyaki
Thai Style Curried Chicken
Egg Foo Yung (suitable for vegetarians)
Stir Fried Vegetables with an Oyster Sauce
Fragrant Steamed Rice

★   ★   ★

DESSERT

A selection of Exotic Sorbets including Mango, Pawpaw and Pineapple,
arranged in Tropical Fruit Shells and decorated with Lychees
Toffee Bananas

★   ★   ★

Coffee, Jasmine Tea, Chocolates and Fortune Cookies

# CHAPTER 4
# Canapés

Anyone experienced in planning wedding receptions will probably confirm the belief that the only simple method of eating while standing up is to be offered food that can be picked up with the fingers and eaten in one go. The scope for this sort of food is virtually endless and canapés represent a wonderfully creative opportunity for combining texture and taste with visual presentation which some caterers have made into an art all of their own.

The term 'canapés' has two interpretations. For many hotels and some outside caterers, 'canapés' refers to things passed around prior to a meal, consisting mainly of bread or pastry bases topped with something fishy, cheesy or in the pâté line. They will often be highly garnished and sometimes glazed with aspic to stop the food from drying out.

For the majority of outside caterers, 'canapés' refers simply to all types of food passed round and offered by waiters and waitresses and designed to be picked from the tray and eaten more or less in a couple of bites. Canapés can be served as appetisers before a meal or served as a replacement to a meal in which case they will need to be much more substantial. The essential point to remember is that guests have freedom of movement and circulation and at no stage are required to juggle plates and cutlery. If anyone refers to 'canapés', make sure you know which interpretation they are basing the discussions on, as the requirements and considerations bear little resemblance to each other. Canapés are sometimes referred to as a 'finger buffet', the only exception being that in this case the food may actually be laid out rather than passed around and guests may be given little plates. The content of the food can be pretty much the same and will still be eaten with the fingers.

Canapés can be chosen to fit a theme – everything heart-shaped is a common if rather clichéd example. They can be chosen to include elements of the cuisine of all sorts of different cultures to provide variety and interest. They can be hot or cold, savoury or sweet or designed to suit a particular time of day. Brochettes of tiny sausages, cherry tomatoes, mushrooms and bacon, or of fresh exotic fruits, or miniature warm croissants filled with Gruyère would be ideal for breakfasts served late into the night to keep guests going. Tiny sandwiches and little chocolate éclairs, fruit tarts, miniature meringues and buttered crumpets cut to bite size with a pastry cutter are perfect for afternoon tea. Spicy chicken satays with peanut dip, Oriental prawns or oysters in the shell with lime juice and chopped chives will add an adventurous flair to canapés at any time of the day or night.

Whether designed to whet the appetite for what is to come or to be substantial enough so that nothing needs to follow, a good caterer will be able to give you endless ideas and help you put together a canapé menu to suit the tastes and hunger of your guests.

The Admirable Crichton is a catering company with a far-reaching reputation for originality and flair in their choice and presentation of canapés. Johnny Roxburgh, design director to The Admirable Crichton, has a view of canapés and their presentation which has changed over the last few years – ostentation and flamboyance are a thing of the past and although lots of weddings are still the perfect time to produce tiny bite-sized treats arranged on flower and leaf filled baskets there is a definite trend towards understated, simple trays of food which tastes wonderful, light and imaginative.

Plain, thick sheets of Perspex look superb as the foil to Italian bruschetta, with basil, mozzarella and deep red ribbons of sundried tomatoes – summery and clean. Black slate or hollowed out vegetables are easy to carry and waiters can move simply through tightly packed guests. The secret of inventive containers is to take improbable objects and use them courageously. Colanders, bathracks, terracotta flower pots – scrubbed clean and lined with linen napkins, even the humblest tray can be used successfully.

Canapés should be small and neat – they shouldn't drip or drop and neither should they leave the person eating them with a tail, claw or bone as an embarrassing reminder of what they have just eaten. Only one kind should be on a tray and preferably not arranged in depressingly complicated patterns. When replenished the trays should always be cleaned – it's dreadful to have the marks on the surface left by the last round of canapés.

Most importantly there should always be enough – guests get dressed at 12 o'clock, drive two hours into the country, sit for an hour in the church – when they get to the reception at 4 o'clock they're hungry. The final tip for success: make sure the waiters get to the back of the room. A hungry guest is not generally a relaxed one.

---

## Summer Wedding Canapés

*Served Hot*:

Carpaccio of Tuna with Salsa Verde on Brioche

Thai style Fish Cakes with a Cucumber Relish

Eggs Benedict – Poached Quail's Egg on a toasted Muffin with Smoked Salmon and Hollandaise Sauce

Parmesan and Gruyère Beignet rolled in Pecorino

Baby Tomato Tarte Tatin

*Served Cold*:

Crostini with Goat's Cheese, Pesto and Pecan Nuts

Caesar Salad – Crisp Bacon, Quail's Egg, Anchovy and Lettuce in Parmesan Dressing on a Croustade

Sushi with Smoked Salmon and Wasabi

Heart-shaped Scones topped with lashings of Clotted Cream and Strawberry Jam

Tiny Peanut Butter and Chocolate Chip Cookie, Vanilla Ice Cream Sandwich

# Christmas Wedding Canapés

*Served Hot*:

Pan fried Fois Gras on a Corn Fritter

Molten Stilton and Pear on a Croute

Smoked Goose and Apple Strudel

Piroshki filled with Wild Mushrooms

Roast Turkey, Parsnip Purée and Cranberries piled high on a
Sage and Onion stuffing Croute

Hot sweet Cinnamon Toast

*Served Cold*:

Venison Carpaccio and Juniper-scented Jelly on Brioche

Smoked Salmon crackers filled with Beetroot and Celeriac Remoulade

Pistachio Wafer with Creamy Stilton and a Tangerine Chutney

Walnut and Caraway Biscotti with smoked Duck and
Cranberry Chutney

# CHAPTER 5
# The Venue

You will by now have come to some decision as to the type and style of wedding reception you would like to have. Your next task will be to decide where it might be held.

## 1. At home

This should be the starting point for all brides. Home might mean your own or that of your parents, a member of your family or a close friend. A wedding reception that is held at home is always personal.

Few families are lucky enough to be able to consider all types of reception at home, but many could consider a traditional teatime or canapés reception, perhaps using several rooms in the house together. Being practical, there is nothing wrong with spreading your guests between various rooms but you will want to think about whether you might have a space large enough for everyone to assemble together to listen to speeches and witness you cut the cake.

For most families, the opportunity to hold a wedding reception at home will involve the hiring of a marquee. If this is likely to apply to you, turn now to page 92 to find out what you will need to bear in mind in making the choice of marquee.

Wedding receptions held at home, apart from being intensely personal events, also have other advantages. The first and probably most important of these is that you remain in control of every detail and cost to do with your wedding. Many reception venues will have tied catering, some will insist upon the use of particular florists, photographers and entertainers. There may be perfectly acceptable reasons for this insistence upon recommended suppliers. In a built up area, for example, a reception venue will have to comply with noise restrictions imposed by the local environmental office to ensure that local residents are not disturbed by music and dancing that goes on late. As a result, they may prefer to work only with entertainers and bands who they know will obey these restrictions. Other cases of imposed subcontraction may not be based on such

worthy principles and can mean simply that a commission is
passed back to the source of recommendation and this is
something you should watch out for, question and be prepared
to argue about.

## 2. Hotels

Most brides choose a particular wedding reception venue on
the basis of the attractiveness of the setting or location and this
is a normal and natural starting point. However, no matter
how lovely a setting might be, other elements will greatly
influence how successful your wedding day will be. A pretty
hotel is not necessarily competent. In order to enjoy planning
your wedding, the staff must be helpful and sensitive to your
wishes and preferences and be prepared to work for their
money. The sort of relationship you enjoy with the staff of
your reception venue during the planning of your wedding will
affect your enjoyment of the day itself and you should get a
pretty good idea of the level of service you can expect early on.
If for any reason staff are inflexible in their approach or
unhelpful, you would do better to look elsewhere.

Working with hotel staff towards a wedding reception can be
very helpful to a busy bride. Most banqueting managers will
be experienced at running and coordinating the reception side
of weddings. They will often be full of advice and may well
have creative suggestions to add to your own. The role of the
banqueting manager is specifically to liaise between the client
and the kitchen. Some are excellent, others are atrocious, and
in the draw you must carefully investigate this before placing
your reception at any hotel.

The subject of room hire charges for hotel receptions needs
some discussion. Some will impose a room hire charge as a
matter of course, others will only look for a fee if the room
which could seat a large number of guests is used only for a
small number. Other instances where you might be expected
to pay room charges are if you want a reception or dance to go
on beyond a certain time limit at night, or if the timing of your
reception (for example a late lunch) means that the hotel is
unable to use the room again that day for another client. You
must remember that you will be paying the hotel the significant cost attached to whatever you have planned for your
guests and brides must always feel able to negotiate all such
extra costs. Furthermore, using the hotel facilities for your

reception, you should be able to negotiate favourable bedroom rates for any guests who might wish to stay there. You may even be offered a complimentary night in the hotel yourself. Haggling costs is a very non-British trait but it can sometimes be quite successful.

Menus submitted by hotels for wedding receptions will most often be an all-in price, including service and furniture and whatever equipment is necessary and usually VAT as well. This is rarely the case when you request menus from an outside caterer because until a caterer knows the individual requirements of a site, they are unable to know what equipment, if any, is needed. This does not necessarily make a reception held at a hotel cheaper than one held elsewhere but is an important point to remember whilst comparing prices of menus.

Hotel wines are generally more expensive than those supplied either in restaurants or by outside caterers. This is no small consideration when you have a large number of guests. Wedding receptions where wine is limited can be very dull for the guests. Always try to negotiate the price of wines, especially if by choosing to provide your own, you are asked to pay a high corkage.

Hotels will sometimes offer clients an all-inclusive price for the food and wine. To a client concerned with cost, this is a naturally attractive idea but you MUST be very wary. Wine allowances will rarely be generous and even close friends may be unlikely to tell you that while your top table was served with unlimited, good quality wine and champagne, guests on other tables only received limited quantities of horrible wine. If you are considering an all-inclusive package, you must have assurances of what and how much will be offered to your guests.

Most hotels provide good food. Always try to talk to the chef personally about the menu you would like him or her to prepare for you and be specific. If you, as a client, show your interest and enthusiasm it does filter through. Always ask for a menu sampling once you have chosen your menu just to be sure that what is served is what you are expecting, right down to the details of the way in which vegetables are cut, cooked and served. You should not be charged separately for this unless the number of guests you are expecting at the reception is too small to allow enough profit to be generated by your reception to cover the cost of a sample lunch or dinner.

Be careful with timings for a hotel wedding reception. Sometimes there will be an extra charge for going on late or monopolising a room and thereby preventing the hotel from using it again that day. Always make sure that you know how this will affect your plans. The last thing you want is to be forced to leave your own wedding earlier than anticipated or to be suddenly expected to pay unknown costs. You only have yourself to blame if this is not discovered at an early stage.

## 3. Other venues

Brides are often surprised to discover just how many alternatives to hotels are available as wedding reception venues and quite what a wide variety these represent. Public buildings, civic amenities and halls connected to a religious establishment are perhaps the most obvious. Details of civic facilities available for hire in a particular area are available from the local borough authority. Ministers of churches and synagogues will be able to advise couples of halls to which they might have access for receptions.

### THE NATIONAL TRUST

The National Trust owns a large number of houses and stately homes throughout the United Kingdom, many of which can be hired for wedding receptions. The Trust has a very useful book for anyone considering hiring a property of this sort giving contact names and telephone numbers, details of facilities and restrictions and limitations of use, entitled *Wining and Dining in Historic Houses* and this is available on request.

A couple of points should be made if you are considering this as an option. Most of the Trust-owned properties are open to the public during the day, therefore receptions are often limited to evenings only. Because of the often priceless buildings and contents, insurance restrictions can sometimes prevent smoking, red wine and dancing in certain areas. Dancing may well require a marquee in the inevitably beautiful grounds and this can end up being an expensive venue choice and one that should not be considered by brides working to a limited budget. The same restrictions and limitations are likely to apply to any hired house, whether it belongs to the National Trust or any other private individual or heritage group.

BOATS

Wherever you live, if it is close to a river, lake or the sea, you will find that there are companies who will operate boats for all sorts of uses. Many of these, particularly river operators, will have boats available for receptions ranging from modern cruisers to original paddlesteamers. A wedding reception or part of it on board can be great fun, particularly since it gives you an immediate and easy theme to introduce to other areas of the wedding. Details of river operators will normally be available from river or port authorities.

MUSEUMS, GALLERIES AND GARDENS

Every city and large town in the United Kingdom hides a wealth of interesting places which can be hired for receptions. During the 1980s, the huge growth of corporate hospitality meant that almost any location, private or public, took steps to capitalise on income which could be generated by the hiring of facilities to corporate clients. This has indirectly benefited brides looking for interesting venues in which to hold their wedding receptions because although the corporate market has been a little more rationalised, the facilities which were established as professional operations are in most cases still available and keen for business of any kind.

The type of locations to look out for could be any of the following:

Art galleries
Zoos
Botanical gardens
Centres of historic interest
Museums
Privately-owned houses
Headquarters of societies and institutions
Conference centres
Armed forces headquarters

One excellent way to find out about facilities in a particular area is to contact the local tourist authority. They will be able to send you information on most of the above categories. They may also have dealt with and therefore know various conference organisers who could help you in your search. If you find the thought too daunting, remember that wherever you are, there will probably be caterers, party planners and even the odd wedding specialist who will be well used to the problems you are encountering and will be able to smooth your path.

## CLUBS AND SPORTING VENUES

Families will often consider holding a wedding reception at the sporting, country or social club to which a member belongs. The same advice applies to these as to hotels. Make sure you know what you are getting, try it and taste it and ask as many questions as you need in order to see exactly how it will work for the best. You cannot expect too much from a club. It is there purely to offer a basic service to its members and is not likely to be as versatile or creative as most hotels and outside catering firms.

## VENUES FOR COMBINING CIVIL CEREMONIES WITH RECEPTIONS

Many hotels, clubs, reception venues, National Trust properties and local authority run buildings have now been granted licences to hold civil marriages. Whilst we are primarily concerned in this section with matters relating to the wedding reception, you would be wise to have an understanding of the legal restrictions and practical implications if you are considering combining your ceremony and reception under one roof. Application for a wedding licence will usually be considered if the venue meets certain criteria. The venue must be generally open to the public. It must be a permanent structure with a roof. Gardens, even of licensed venues, may not be used for civil marriages. It must have no religious connections in its past and no religious connotations or artefacts in the room in which marriages are to take place, for example any stained glass in the windows would rule it out. The building's use and administration must be 'seemly and dignified', as befitting a place in which a legal contract is, after all, being made. Licences are renewable after three years. The law prohibits the serving of food or drink in the room in which the marriage is to take place for one hour before the ceremony is due to start. You may not feel that providing refreshments before the ceremony is necessary and you would most probably be right, however you must consider seating your guests during the marriage. In either of these cases sufficient space must be available, preferably with a separate room for the actual marriage so that the celebrations can begin after the ceremony without chairs having to be moved away. You can apply to any Town Hall for a list of local venues licensed to hold civil marriages and since the 1994 Marriage Act has lifted the long-standing residency rules, couples are now free to marry in any area. Many of these venues are unusual and exciting places to plan a wedding and there can be great scope for creativity, so they are well worth investigating if you know you will have a civil ceremony.

## 4. The great outdoors – Marquees

From a straightforward plastic roof awning to a custom-built palace of a tent, the word 'marquee' hides such a multitude of different meanings that in spite of thousands being erected and dismantled every year, they remain one of the least understood areas of a wedding.

Let us start with the basics. To most of us, a marquee means

a canvas structure, held up by poles in the tent, tensioned by ropes set into the ground around the marquee – the kind of thing we would associate with a country fête. This is a traditional pole tent and for many years was the only type of marquee generally available. In the last twenty years or so, technology has made its impact upon the marquee industry like so many others. Referring again to the corporate hospitality trade, the demands made upon marquee manufacturers and suppliers to fulfil the needs of larger groups of guests in increasingly difficult locations led to a vastly improved choice of tent structure and type and the development of the frame tent. A frame tent is one which is based upon a metal structure of component parts which fit together to make an infinite variety of shapes and sizes. Because the metal structure supports the weight of the canvas (or in some cases heavy duty plastic), no poles or ropes are needed and the space within the tent is therefore clear and no space is required around the tent itself for ropes.

Most contemporary marquee suppliers concentrate on frame rather than pole tents for obvious reasons. They are more durable, more versatile and easier to keep in good condition. They can also be erected in sites where space is limited. Some older marquee firms will still use their pole tents but in general these are becoming more difficult to find and are slowly becoming phased out. Frame tents are rarely as high in the apex as pole tents and seldom look as pretty from the outside. Many marquee suppliers would be surprised if you specifically asked for a pole tent, assuming you would automatically want the more modern equipment. Do not be put off if a traditional pole tent appeals to you. They may not be so modern but they have a charm all of their own.

A marquee is not a fully-equipped structure in itself. It comes, like a house, in component parts and each part is costed separately. With the addition of every component, the total price can be substantial. However not every component is needed for every wedding and this is where brides will often be pleasantly surprised that they can actually afford to have a marquee. Marquees involve:

Basic structure;
Lining for walls and ceiling;
Matting or boarding and carpeting for floor;

   Lighting;
   Heating;
   Furniture.

Before you approach a marquee company for a quotation for your wedding tent, you must know what you are intending to use it for and for how long. Why pay for expensive lighting in a tent that is only intended to be used informally for a bright summer's afternoon? If you are planning to use the tent at night for dancing following the reception, then you will have to consider not only the lighting of the tent, but heating it too. The costs which can be cut for a marquee to be used in the summer are very different from the expensive considerations of a marquee for a winter wedding.

   Marquee quotations can be difficult to understand and misleading. So many families confirm bookings with marquee companies on the basis of quotations supplied months in advance which may well not include additional costs which themselves only become subjects for discussion far closer to the time. They may not have understood that essential lighting or heating or necessary boarding to the floor of the tent are not included in the quotation to which they will have budgeted. Not by any stretch of the imagination could it be assumed that marquee suppliers will always bring your attention to these areas of hidden cost. You must know what it is you need and how much it will cost from the outset.

   In order to generate a profit, marquee suppliers need to achieve a certain number of bookings during any one year. Every extra booking is greater profit. There will be an optimum number of times any one marquee structure should be hired out in any one season while still leaving time to repair and clean it between bookings. If the opportunity arises to hire out a marquee once more than is ideal, who can blame a company for trying to capitalise on this? It is up to you to insist that your tent is clean and tidy and if necessary be prepared to argue the case if it is not. It is logical to point out that these problems will be most likely to occur towards the end of a busy summer season although this is not always the case. If you know that your tent is for use towards the end of the summer you should pay particular attention to this point and establish what the state of the marquee will be early on.

   There is a huge difference in the quality and price of

marquees offered by different suppliers and, within reason, you do get what you pay for. For this reason, if you are considering hiring a marquee, you must get at least three comparable quotations. Many families think that the most reasonably priced marquee is likely to come from a local supplier. This is not necessarily the case at all. Many of the largest and most exclusive and luxurious marquee companies are based in the country rather than the town. If a bride's mother, looking for a simple garden tent, was to approach any of these, she would probably be so shocked by the price that she would abandon any further hope of affording a marquee at all. If she only knew that by going a little further afield she could get a cheaper quotation. There is no reason why a marquee company cannot travel a little distance without this adding significantly to the cost of the tent. It is, after all, a case of a truck and some strong arms.

Finally, on the general discussion of marquees, it is important to know when the tent is to be put up and when it will be taken away again. Obviously, florists and caterers need to have time to do their work and you cannot have tables being laid by staff while florists are rushing around with ladders trying to decorate tent poles. Marquees erected on grass will take a toll on the health of the grass underneath and while a little damage must be expected and is a small price to pay for a glorious wedding, you will not want the tent up any longer than necessary.

## MARQUEE LININGS

Linings are usually available in a variety of colours and styles and are designed to hide the structure of the tent and give warmth and colour to the interior, rather like wallpaper. Lining is either applied flat to the walls, pleated or ruched and tends to come in stripes of white and a colour or as a flat colour. Some marquee companies used striped tent structures so as to avoid the need for lining. While these are certainly more attractive than unlined ordinary tents, they do not compare with proper lining in look, since the structure of the tent remains visible most of the time. Brides often choose pastel shades of lining to suit wedding colours, but for the sake of individuality, they could consider a more vivid colour scheme. Having everything in a pastel shade can be very bland and it is easy to lose depth and form. Marquee suppliers should be able to provide samples of linings as well as photographs to show what the linings actually look like when attached and there is often a considerable difference.

## Marquee Floorings

A marquee erected on a flat, well-drained piece of grass and intended for use during the summer would not, in most cases, need a boarded floor. Matting, usually made from coconut fibre, is quite enough to protect the grass underneath and provide a good surface to walk on. It is normally plastic lined to prevent damp seeping up from underneath. Many marquee suppliers only provide matting in a very bright red colour which can intrude terribly upon gentler colour schemes and in general does not look very nice. If this is important to you, ask about more neutral alternatives, even if it does entail a little extra cost.

A boarded floor is essential to a marquee that needs to be erected on an uneven piece of ground. Bumps are not just difficult, they can be dangerous to you and your guests. Boarded floors are time-consuming to lay and therefore expensive. Once boarded the floor is then usually carpeted, or in some cases laid over simply with matting.

Marquees are most often associated with summer weddings, for obvious reasons. They are, if approached correctly, just as appropriate for winter weddings but a different set of rules must apply to your approach. The only way to insulate a marquee against the cold and to keep the necessary heat in, is to board and carpet the floor, however flat the ground might be. Walls, too, must be double-lined and these factors alone can mean a winter marquee being greatly more expensive.

## Marquee Lighting

Most marquee companies will supply quotations for tents with a consideration made for lighting of some sort. This price will usually include plugging one or perhaps two extension leads into an electricity supply close by which will power the lights. It is not likely to include the cost or work involved in getting the electricity supply to a distant site, so beware.

Marquee lighting can take the form of chandeliers and similar wall brackets or more modern types of pinspots and uplighters. The atmosphere created by different types of lighting is important and even on a dimmer switch, chandeliers and wall brackets are rarely as moody and intimate. If your marquee supplier cannot supply the type of lighting you would like, do not abandon hope for there are plenty of specialist lighting companies who will, but you will need to allow for this extra cost. Firms which supply discotheques and entertainment can often help with lighting. You may need a certain amount of lighting even during the day in summer.

One marquee hire firm with a reputation for attentive service and beautifully clean and tidy tents is Inside Outside Marquee Hire. Frank Batty gives us his thoughts:

---

### FRANK BATTY – INSIDE OUTSIDE MARQUEE HIRE

The secret to the success of a good party lies in the preparation. The more detailed the planning, the greater the event. As an organiser and/or host, it is the forethought, the organisation, and all the small decisions along the way which will ultimately set the individual atmosphere unique to every occasion.

When planning a wedding reception, whether it is to be an informal finger buffet for a handful of family and friends, or a dinner dance to entertain every branch of the family tree and all of their/your friends, one has to start with the basics. This is where the marquee contractor can provide help and advice through practical experience.

> How many guests will there be?
> Will all the guests be served at tables?
> Will there be dancing, a band or a disco?
> Is a buffet area required?
> Will there be a bar area?
> Would a reception area be needed?

The answers to these questions will determine how much space is required. (The only thing worse than being surrounded by cold empty spaces at a supposedly intimate shoulder-rubbing bash, is, of course, rubbing shoulders in a hot dinner dance marquee in full evening dress!)

Very often, getting a caterer involved to help from the start is a good idea, since they will be looking after things on the big day, and the more information the marquee contractor has through liaising, the more effectively he can organise layout, style and services. Most professional caterers have no wish to burden the prospective brides' parents with details of power requirements, preparation tables needed etc., so a good working relationship can forestall many a headache, and avoid any unpleasant surprises when it is too late.

Once the basic marquee size is decided, a site survey is carried out. This not only gives the marquee contractor an opportunity to advise on what may be necessary (i.e. a sub-floor is necessary on certain surfaces, an area may need levelling, or a flower bed may be made into a feature, or a tree included within the marquee etc.) but also it is important to meet with the family to glean a personal 'feel' for how they would like things done.

The fun begins for the bride/client at this point, for now comes the choices only she/they can make. The colour scheme, material type, plain or fancy, lighting style and even interior themes will all effect a personalised character to the setting.

As marquee contractors, we can readily envisage people's ideas, and advise and guide as to what won't work, and improve on ideas that will.

In real life, as we all know, nothing is perfect or easy, and rarely does a client know exactly what they want, since organising a wedding is not a regular occurrence. It is the skill and expertise of the marquee contractor to make provisions and judgements, to guide the practical aspects smoothly and without fuss to a relaxed and memorable conclusion – right down to leaving nothing behind but a slightly yellow shape on the lawn where memories were once the reality.

*Candles*

Candlelight is lovely but it can also be extremely dangerous, especially in a marquee. Never, ever use candles that are placed at a level or in a position where they can be knocked over by people and movement unless they are somehow encased in a container. Little nightlights in glass or terracotta pots are usually fine because flowers and sleeves are protected from the flame and if the pots are knocked over, the flame will go out. Large candelabra placed on tables, where the first candle starts at a sufficient height above the heads of the guests are in most cases also acceptable. Any other unprotected flame on a table or anywhere else represents a serious fire risk and you must be aware of the danger. A marquee can burn down in a matter of seconds. Be sensible, be safe, be happy.

If a wedding reception is to take place in a marquee, the marquee itself may not be the only area needing to be lit. Walkways and pathways to the house or to loos or to cars parked in distant fields will need some lighting too. Sometimes the marquee firm will be able to help with this. At other times you would be better advised to approach a professional lighting firm. In any case there are some creative tricks you can employ yourself.

Pea-lights are the name for what we normally associate with Christmas trees. Plain bulbs set either on a constant or on a flicker look lovely in any tree or bush and even in flower arrangements in the marquee. It is possible to buy strings of battery-operated pea-lights which make their use even easier. A string of such bulbs will cost you just a few pounds and will come in useful for all sorts of parties and of course at Christmas. You can generally find these lights in those funny little mail order catalogues which always arrive inside the Sunday papers.

For a wedding that is to take place in a garden setting, families can easily be persuaded to spend the preceding months collecting jam jars, pickle jars and any other clear glass pots that would normally be thrown away. When cleaned thoroughly, labels peeled, these make excellent and free containers in which to place candles all around the garden. They can be wired at the lip to be attached to tree branches or simply placed among flower beds and along paths for a really magical look. Only ever use old, unwanted pots for this purpose as many will take months to retrieve and inevitably some are cracked or lost in the process. Other simple lighting ideas for gardens are strings of ordinary coloured bulbs either stretched across the garden, or set into branches and Chinese paper lanterns. If you use the ordinary candles which are usually provided with paper lanterns, you will find that they have a terrible tendency to catch fire. Replace these with nightlights in aluminium sleeves by placing one full sleeve inside another empty one and attach the empty one to the metal supports inside the lantern. Paper lanterns should only ever be used outside.

## MARQUEE ADDITIONS

Unless you can join a marquee directly on to a house, you will need some sort of walkway of protection, or awning, for you and your guests in case of heavy rain. Awnings are priced on required lengths and again need to be lit at night. The roof can be lined to match the marquee.

## SERVICE TENTS

These are usually very basic canvas structures that either butt up to, or are situated close by the main marquee. They are, as the name suggests, for the use of the staff, either as a kitchen in which case it will need to be fully equipped, or as a service and clearing area. You will only know what size of service tent you require and whether in fact you require one at all after speaking to your caterer. A service tent that cannot connect directly with the main tent will need awning to attach it. Staff can occasionally be allowed to get wet but certainly not the food!

## ELECTRICITY

This will in most cases be drawn from a house or point of supply close by. Depending on how much power is required, this will come from a simple 13 amp socket using an extension lead or in more difficult cases straight from the fuse box. If a marquee is situated too far for extension leads, a generator will be required to power any form of lighting at all. Generators come in all sorts of shapes and sizes and you can usually find companies who supply these in the local telephone directory. They can be noisy so you will want to discuss how best to avoid the disturbance.

Lighting is not the only drain on electricity supply. Any form of heating or cooking that requires it must be taken into account in assessing how much power you need. Discotheques and bands may need it too. Even an electrically-operated boiling urn requires a surprisingly large amount of electricity, so do consult your caterer. Old houses or those without modern wiring can have problems with trip switches, so be aware of these requirements.

## LOOS

There is a realistic limit to how far you can expect your guests to have to walk to get to a loo. If the marquee is close to the house, the facilities inside will usually do. If not, you should consider a temporary loo of some sort. From the very basic to the unbelievably glamorous, portable loos are available to suit the occasion. The very basic are not so nice and do tend to splash the flush all over you which can be most aggravating when you are smartly dressed. The new wave of glamorous portable loos are expensive by comparison, but definitely lend a better air to the nose-powdering experience.

## DANCE FLOORS

Any marquee in which you would like to dance will need a dance floor as it is just not possible to dance properly without one. Most marquee suppliers will be able to provide dance floors, failing which the band or discotheque you are using should be able to help. Always make sure that it is large enough for the number of guests you anticipate. Dance floors can also be useful before the dancing as a covered area on which you could have drinks during the reception if it is raining.

## STAGES

If you are having a particularly large marquee, or are planning any form of entertainment, it is a good idea to investigate a stage at one end, which will equally well be used for speeches and cake cutting. Marquee companies will normally be able to supply these at a low cost.

## MARQUEE SIZES

When you approach a marquee supplier for a quotation, it is wise to have a good idea of the size you need so that you know you are being sold the right thing.

Remember that you obtain the square footage of a space by multiplying the length by the breadth. A marquee that is 60' × 40' will give you a square footage of 2400 square feet. The following figures give guidelines on the minimum space allowance per guest, according to the type of reception.

| *Style* | Sq ft per guest req. |
|---|---|
| Canapés, stand up, no seating | 6–8 |
| Canapés, stand up, some seating | 8–10 |
| Teatime, some seating | 8–10 |

| Lunch/dinner fully seated – rectangular tables | 10–12 |

| Lunch/dinner fully seated – round tables of<br>10 (5' in diameter) | 12–16 |

| as above, tables of 6 or 8 (4' round) | 12–16 |

| as above, tables of 10 to 12 (6' round) | 12–16 |

| Cathedral seating, in rows<br>(e.g. for Jewish ceremony) | 6–8 |

| Dance floor | 2–4 |

If you are working to a fixed area or space and you want to know how many guests you can fit in, divide the square footage of the room by the number of square feet required per guest from the table above, to get the capacity. NB, if you are intending to dance, remember to add the requirements for the dance floor as a separate calculation.

Table sizes and seating capacities

| Type | Size | Seats |
| --- | --- | --- |
| Rectangular trestle | 6' × 2.5' | 6–8 |
| Rectangular trestle | 8' × 2.5' | 8–10 |
| Round | 4' | 6–8 |
| Round | 5' | 8–10 |
| Round | 6' | 10–12 |

Space is important for comfort, so wherever possible, use the smaller figure.

## Serving Space Allowances

You will need to allow space for access for staff from service areas. Always allow at least 4ft between round tables for chairs, guests and staff and, if possible, 5ft between rectangular tables where the seating is back to back. This allows 2ft for serving staff and 1.5ft for a chair containing a person.

## 5. Security

Professional security guards are an invaluable asset to any celebration and particularly to one held in a marquee or house which is open for guests to wander in and out. There is always a risk that the busy wedding preparations will not have missed the criminal element in any area and stories abound of families whose weddings are ruined by crime. Cars parked for convenience in fields are sitting targets as are houses left open and unwatched. You will also be legally responsible for the safekeeping of any equipment hired to you for the wedding, so it is up to you to keep it secure.

## 6. Rubbish

For anyone not greatly experienced in the debris produced by even a small party, it is difficult to imagine quite how much rubbish is produced by a larger celebration. In your own interests, you should discuss the forthcoming wedding with your local dustbin men and ask whether, for a small token of your gratitude, they might be persuaded to cope with all the extra work. If they cannot help or are not interested in doing so, you will need to think about hiring a mini skip, which is relatively inexpensive and can usually be found in the local telephone directory. If placed on a public road, a skip needs a licence, although the company concerned will normally be able to organise this for you. As a last resort, you may have to persuade a group of friends or relatives to remove the rubbish after the wedding to the municipal dump and take the bottles to the bottle bank, but this is a revolting job and one that is to be avoided if at all possible.

## 7. Parking for guests

Even a reasonably small wedding reception can lead to the appearance of a large number of cars, all of which need to be left securely somewhere. If your reception is being held in a hotel, you will probably find the solution to this problem easily in discussion with your banqueting manager. For any wedding held at home, you might need to throw yourself on the mercy of neighbours and farmers for permission to use drives, car parks and fields. Think about how easy it will be for people to park in fields if it is wet and muddy and how secure their cars and contents are likely to be. You must also consider how guests might find their cars in the dark and plan to light the path at least to a reasonable degree.

For a little advice and some helpful tips for venue problem solving, over to Searcy's, one of London's oldest catering firms.

### Atmosphere of a Venue

- What is your first impression? Remember it because that is what your guests will see with their 'fresh eyes'. Don't forget what your initial reaction to the venue was once you've visited it a dozen times.

- However, if your first impression was that the room felt empty or lacking in atmosphere, remember that it will look different, more welcoming when it is furnished and your guests have arrived.

- Think of the colours: look for, or add, warm and rich colours for winter and cool, pale tones for summer.

- Is the venue jaded? Have there been just too many parties there before yours? Are the staff too blasé?

- Does the venue feel 'happy'? Consider not just the atmosphere of the place but the attitude and enthusiasm of the people running it. Do they care? Are they careful enough? Will they pay enough attention to detail FOR YOU?

- Although it's hard to be anything but subjective, look at the style – of the decor, the facilities, the management and staff. Do they match your expectations? Do they have the style and flair you expect?

- Are they experienced enough? Will you feel COMPLETELY relaxed on the day, safe in the knowledge that they will carry out your instructions to the letter and even anticipate your wishes before you do?

### What Does it Need to Turn it into Your Dream?

| Problem | Solution |
| --- | --- |
| It's too big. | Use à tent lining to reduce the space, possibly even a roof lining only. |
| It's too small. | Arrange a marquee extension built to match the interior. Use smaller tables – round tables of 8 are more space efficient and more intimate than tables of 10 guests. |

| There's insufficient space for guests to wait, out of the elements, before being received. | Add tent awnings to extend the room. |
|---|---|
| Generally lacking in atmosphere. | Consult a specialist lighting company to focus pinspots of light on the flowers on each table – breathtaking for evening parties. |
| It's too bare. | Use coloured tablecloths, lots of flowers and lighting. Nowadays even hotels allow this. |
| The standard of catering isn't good enough for you. | Ask if you can 'buy out' the catering – it may not be more expensive – and import your own. |

Searcy's own private house for hire at 30 Pavillion Road is an absolutely beautiful venue that requires very little enhancement with flowers or lighting, in fact it can be *over*-decorated easily. With our years of catering experience in over 70 other venues for hire and in hundreds of private homes each year one truth *always* emerges: it is the people that really make a party but at the same time the layout and the atmosphere of the venue is the very next most important contributory factor in a reception's success. However, do take account of what your Venue Manager recommends, particularly in relation to how people move *around* a venue. This does have an effect on how the layout will work and that kind of knowledge comes only from experience gained working in a venue on a daily basis.

## CHAPTER 6
# Ancillary Services

## 1. Furniture

Once you have your marquee, you must equip it. This applies to marquees rather than other forms of reception venue, which are more likely to be equipped already, but this is something you will want to be sure of. Marquee companies will often be able to supply the furniture and sometimes all the equipment necessary, including cutlery, china, glasses, linen and bar needs. If a marquee company actually owns the equipment they are offering to you, then the price per item will be competitive. Many will simply hire in what you require from specialist hire companies and place a mark up on the price at which they buy it before selling it on to you, in which case you would have been better off approaching the hire company directly. Do investigate and compare prices.

## 2. Hired equipment

Every single item you hire down to the last teaspoon and champagne glass will cost money. While all hire companies will help you establish an overall budgeting figure for hired equipment for your wedding, until you have decided exactly what you are serving in terms of both food and drink, this figure is subject to change. Depending on the style of reception chosen, the cost of hired equipment can be a significant part of the overall drain on your budget and you need to bear this in mind. Start from a logical point. A hot meal needs cooking equipment. Catering-sized ovens are expensive to hire. Do not be afraid to discuss this point with your caterers. They will be able to advise on menu suggestions which can be served hot without the need to invest in massive quantities of costly industrial ovens and hot cupboards. Hired equipment covers a wide range of different styles and patterns of cutlery, china and glassware and you should ask to see samples of what is currently in use by any company you are intending to use. Most china used for celebrations is plain white with a gold or silver edge. Most cutlery is Kings pattern in either stainless steel or silver plate. As always, make sure you know what you are booking and what the alternatives might be.

### 3. Glasses

Certain drinks should be served in certain types of glasses and this is something that any professional in the world of catering or wines should be fully aware of. Few people, whether amateur or professional would consider serving champagne in a tumbler, or whisky in a flute but the same cannot always be said for wines and soft drinks.

Red wine must be served in a glass that is large enough to accommodate a decent glassful of wine while still leaving room in the glass for the wine to breathe. A glass for red wine should be larger than a glass for white wine which does not require the same aeration. Water glasses and those to contain soft drinks need to be of a decent size to give a guest a sensible amount of refreshment. Pudding wines, sweeter and richer than most white wines, are not drunk in quantity so a small wine glass is appropriate.

Champagne is normally served in a flute, or to give a very 1920s feel to the wedding, an old-fashioned champagne bowl could be chosen.

Spirits should be served in tumblers, sometimes called 'highballs' and shorter if for spirits served straight, or in 'slim jims' i.e. longer tumblers for spirits served with mixers. Slim jims are often used for soft drinks and sometimes for beers. It is possible to hire pint glasses for beers, but they are not always easy to find.

Port and sticky liqueurs are served in very small glasses, as are sherries, while brandy, like red wine, needs to aerate and to be correct, brandy should be served in a brandy balloon.

Most hire companies stock a good range of glasses. Some will concentrate on fairly basic lines, others will offer anything up to and including expensive crystal. To be avoided at all costs from an aesthetic point of view are what we would associate with wine served in pubs – known as Paris goblets and often actually sporting their measure line painted on the glass. Unless your wedding reception is actually taking place in a pub, which is a different matter entirely, why would you want pub glasses? They are not pretty, they are not large enough except for small quantities of white wine and should not be used for soft drinks or water and never for champagne.

The hiring of equipment for weddings is often left up to the caterer or hotel involved in preparing and serving the food. If, as may well be the case, you have strong feelings as to styles of glasses, china and cutlery, you must make these known to them.

If, for whatever reason, a family decides to go it alone and organise the hired equipment themselves, they should ask for the advice of the professional company they contact, as there are many areas of hired equipment that demand specialist knowledge. One such company that has contributed to this section by preparing some helpful advice is Gorgeous Gourmets.

---

AVOID THE PITFALLS WHEN HIRING EQUIPMENT
FOR YOUR WEDDING

Once you have chosen your caterer, check that they are going to use the style and quality of crockery, cutlery, glassware, linen, furniture etc. that will make your day even more memorable.

At this stage ascertain whether the catering charges include the provision of crockery, cutlery, linen etc. or whether these costs are additional.

If the style they either have or suggest you hire is not to your liking, do not be afraid to say so and either ask them to find a style you like or find a hire company yourself by using 'Yellow Pages' under the Catering Equipment Hire section.

Some caterers will source the equipment you require and order it on your behalf – free of charge, whilst others will make a small charge or add a percentage to the hire cost for providing this service.

To avoid ordering the wrong style of catering equipment or too much of it, thereby increasing the cost of your wedding, follow these simple rules and you will not waste your time or tax the patience of the hire company who is used to dealing with caterers who know exactly what they want to hire.

1. Visit the hire company that, from their brochure or your telephone conversation with them, appear to have the style and quality of equipment that you require.
2. If you ask the hire company for an idea of costs i.e. a quotation, stress right at the beginning of your conversation that at this stage it is only a quotation, as they tend to deal mainly with the trade and are therefore usually taking orders rather than quoting.
3. Give the hire company you choose at least three weeks' notice of the date, approximate numbers and location of your wedding – whether you require delivery, if so – is there parking for the vehicle close to where you want the equipment delivered? Which floor are the goods going to and is there a lift available for use?
4. Final numbers must be given at least three days prior to the date of your wedding.
5. Obtain a quote for any delivery charges, especially if you are considering hiring any furniture or electrical equipment.
6. It is recommended that the crockery, cutlery, glasses etc. are returned in a 'dirty condition', as it will be cheaper than hiring someone to wash it up – it also creates less mess, especially if the caterers are using your kitchen!
7. Check the payment terms and whether VAT is included or not – it makes a big difference. Full payment and a deposit is normally required either before or on delivery. Most quality hirers will accept Access or Visa.
8. It is essential that either you or your caterer is on site to receive the delivery and to check that the hire order is correct.
9. Losses – especially glasses – are inevitable: to minimise these

ensure your caterers pack the goods back in the same boxes in which they were delivered. Keep cutlery separate and, if possible, although they might be dirty, offer to count them in front of the driver collecting the goods – agreeing losses at this stage lessens the resentment factor when the hire company informs you of your total losses and the costs involved.

10. Never pack wet or damp linen back in plastic bags as:
    a) mildew may grow which cannot be removed, which means that you may be charged their full replacement cost – which is over £30 per tablecloth.
    b) If you put linen in bin bags, there have been occasions where these have been thrown out with the rubbish!

11. Always read the hire company Terms and Conditions, which are normally found in their brochure.

12. Make certain that you are adequately insured, as once the goods are in your possession or have been delivered, they are your responsibility until either you return them or the hire company collects them from your property.

## 4. Linen

Your wedding is an important event and the use of linen tablecloths and napkins as opposed to paper or any other equally disposable means should be encouraged, even if you never use it again. Linen is expensive, but worth the cost. Tablecloths are there to provide a hygienic surface on which to eat. Napkins are there to protect the appearance and clothing of guests. There is, frankly, nothing nastier and less ceremonial than disintegrated and wet paper napkins and tablecloths, however informal a look you are trying to achieve. Similarly, if your budget could stretch to it, ask your caterer to ensure that wooden and stainless steel trays are covered with a linen napkin before guests are offered anything from them. Not only does this present a crisp offering, but glasses are steadier and drips are caught.

Paper napkins are perfectly acceptable when served with canapés or with informal barbecue, teatime or party food and should always be offered rather than nothing.

Trestle tables and the kind normally used for parties and receptions are not very attractive and are always best when fully hidden, including the nasty metal legs. Not all caterers or hotels are as appreciative of this fact as they might be, so if you are concerned about having your tables clothed to the ground, you will need to make this point clear. Some caterers have undercloths in all sorts of different colours and patterns and these can look lovely under a crisp white linen top cloth. Bars and buffets should always be 'boxed' to the ground in white linen to give a sort of hospital corner look and keep excess cloth out of the way.

# CHAPTER 7
# Decorations

## 1. Flowers

Wedding flowers offer every bride the chance to personalise the event in a way that is creative and appropriate to the season and budget of the wedding.

Whether used to make a table top look pretty, or in conjunction with statuary, trellising, columns and pedestals, arches, ponds, pools and props of all kinds, flowers can fill an empty space or fit an existing setting or interior.

Wedding flowers can cost whatever a bride wants to or can afford to spend and this means anything from a couple of hundred pounds to tens of thousands and even more. The cost will depend on the choice of florist, the sophistication of the flowers included in the various arrangements and how ambitious a bride decides to be. The more space that needs to be filled or decorated, the more flowers and foliage will be necessary. The more intricate and time-consuming the choice of style, the more costly the price. Brides do not always appreciate just how much work a florist must devote to the popular choices of garlands and arches for entrances, pillars and tables.

Within reason, the choice of flowers available to a florist is governed by seasonal availability. It is of course possible to find almost any flower at any time of year, for a price. How wise a bride is to pick flowers which are out of season is another matter. Weddings are inextricably linked to the seasons and the cycle of life and nature and it has to be considered more appropriate to pick flowers which have a bearing on this. The more rural the area in which the wedding is to take place, the less choice a bride is likely to find to pick from and in general terms, it is better to approach a florist for advice on this point before setting too much importance on the actual content of flower arrangements.

Wedding flowers do need to be approached with the same attention to appropriateness. It would be strange to find elaborate and highly stylised flower arrangements decorating a simple supper buffet tent. It would also be strange to find the

ballroom of a wonderfully luxurious hotel decorated with a few carnations in an up-turned instant coffee lid with a bit of oasis in it. Money spent on flowers and the style of flowers chosen must be in keeping with the overall budget and location. Your guests cannot be allowed to go hungry or thirsty in favour of lavish pedestal arrangements.

There is an enormous difference in the way in which different florists work and their costs. Some florists have made their trade into an art form and rightfully incorporate their reputations and unique skills into their prices. There is a certain defined snobbery in flowers and these highly skilled professionals will prefer to work with flowers that are perhaps unusual or particularly fragrant or beautiful and which are naturally more expensive and exclusive. These artists will create breathtaking arrangements more resemblant of sculpture, often using fruit, shells, interesting natural containers and other products such as bark or spices, or even glitter to achieve the ideal effect. While the shapes of the end result could be anything from natural and loose to highly styled or amusing, no intellectual or financial effort will have been spared in the search for the right look and this is something you do have to pay for.

At the other end of the spectrum are the florists whose use of and approach to flowers is more traditional and basic. They will not be as concerned with exclusive or unusual flowers and will not always have the same creative abilities. It is rather like the difference between using a painter-decorator or an interior designer to decorate your house. The decorator will usually do a good enough job, simply and for not too much money. An interior designer will always cost more but the end result will be a more cohesive and usually more interesting one and may be closer to what you had in mind. The discrepancy between florists is not just financial. What one can achieve another cannot necessarily mimic and there will always be a reason why an expensive florist is expensive. The biggest mistake you can make with flowers and dealing with florists is to expect a traditional and basic florist to be able to produce the same effect as a highly specialised one. Use the right suppliers for the right result and you will always be successful.

It is nice to visit florists and see photographs and examples of their work and the best tip you could be given is to devote a good amount of time to this. You can ask to see samples of flowers so that when something is referred to by its complicated Latin name, such as *Alchemilla mollis*, you can see exactly what is meant. If, as it is produced, you recognise what you have always thought of as a ghastly weed blighting your parents' flower garden, you can answer with a categorical no! or alternatively re-evaluate your attitude. Never accept a proposal if you are not fully sure of the content.

Fragrance, as well as look, is important and fragrant flowers are popular choices with brides, for obvious reasons. All fragrant flowers are much more expensive than others and will eat into a flower budget very quickly, particularly at certain times of the year.

As an economy measure, you should consider limiting the content of fragrant flowers and supplementing their smell with the use of floral-based room sprays. Whatever you do, choose naturally scented sprays and nothing remotely reminiscent of a bathroom. Room sprays are an ideal way of eliminating the rather damp smell that can linger in a marquee. There are sprays along a tropical theme which can mirror anything visually exotic and give force to the inclusion of fruits in flower arrangements. Christmas spice room sprays can also give instant atmosphere to winter weddings. As a rule of thumb, the more expensive the room spray, the more real the smell and it is probably worth visiting a very expensive shop to find the right one.

Scented candles are also lovely, but to fill a large space with the fragrance would break the bank with the number of candles needed. There is also a wide selection of incenses available that have completely removed the whiff of hippie or high church from joss sticks. Do be careful, however, as these are far stronger in smell than room sprays and none could be classified as fresh garden smells. Used correctly, they can impart an exotic element to the wedding, particularly at night. Used wrongly, they can have the same effect as wearing your favourite lambswool jumper to a bonfire party.

Similarly, scented oils, designed for use with reservoirs placed on lightbulbs, can be particularly good for weddings at home. As the lightbulb heats up, the fragrance is slowly released but the strength and character of the fragrance needs a couple of test runs to establish.

Pot pourri, either bought commercially or home made, can be incorporated into the flower arrangements or anywhere at the reception. It can come in very vivid or natural colours which can reflect a chosen colour scheme. In quantity, pot pourri can be strewn over the floor of a marquee in much the same way that Elizabethan weddings used fresh herbs. Fresh herbs, such as rosemary and thyme, strewn on grass release the most wonderful smells as they are crushed underfoot by guests' shoes. Just do remember to be careful about where and how much you scatter – you want to avoid anyone slipping on anything crushed on wooden or stone flooring.

## CONFETTI

The throwing of some sort of confetti over the bride and groom is part of the general association weddings have with fertility symbols and it is certainly logical to accept rice as the most probable ancient form. Many Registrars and religious ministers wage war against the use of paper confetti and with total justification. Bits of paper lying around on pavements and grass are indeed untidy and not wholly ideologically sound.

Rice is a more biodegradable alternative and will certainly find favour with the local wildlife, but should be thrown carefully. No bride wants a face or a cleavage full of hard little bits of rice.

Fresh flower petals are the most decorative alternative and most florists will be happy to provide this for you so long as you make the request sufficiently in advance. There can be no reason for objecting to a liberal sprinkling of fresh, or even dried flower petals. If you do decide to use pot pourri for this, obviously avoid the types which contain whole pine cones or bits of dried fruit peel or lumps of sandalwood.

Arrange for someone to bring your natural confetti to the church or Register Office in little baskets, perhaps tied with some ribbon and for a couple of friends or bridesmaids to stand outside to offer this to the guests as they emerge and thereby prevent them from reaching for a fistful of paper debris. Wet coloured paper confetti is horrible, as it will mark anything it comes into contact with, especially bridal silks.

One of the hardest things to come to terms with about using fresh flowers is the fact that you will be spending money, and in some cases a great deal of money, on flowers which will normally last no longer than 24 hours. Your expenditure can, however, have a slightly longer lasting impact. Make sure that your table centres and movable arrangements go home with your friends and relatives. Staff will always be grateful for the chance to rifle through the larger arrangements for things to take home. Local hospitals and old people's homes will be grateful for contributions you can remember to arrange to have taken round the next day. If many people can enjoy the effort and financial investment, the moral objections many of us have to flower expenditure will be better swallowed. Finally, never forget the possibility of using living, rather than cut, plants. Spring bulbs make good table centres if planted up in lovely baskets in advance of the wedding and will continue to bloom and blossom for some time. These are even things you can do yourself and thoroughly enjoy doing.

A personal recollection is the tremendous effort and care taken by one bride who had not only done all the flowers herself, she had even made her own invitations from hand-made paper into which tiny flowers had been set. At the reception, each guest's place card included a tiny packet of seeds taken from the flowers and plants used in her bouquet, chosen specially to reflect the personality of each guest.

## FLOWERS FOR THE RECEPTION

The type of reception you have chosen to have will help you in your choice of flowers. Budgeting for flowers is difficult – how long is a piece of string? Few brides will have an unlimited budget to spend on decoration and even if they did, the cost of decoration to last just a few hours, however special, should be kept under control.

Before giving too much thought to types of arrangements, first consider the most important areas to decorate.

### Entrances

These are natural areas for decoration since it is always nice to be greeted by a welcoming arrangement of some sort. Remember, though, that entrances are mostly simply passed through en route to the main areas and although the effect of flowers is nice, guests will probably only have time to appreciate the fact of flowers rather than the form, so plenty of variegated foliages studded with just a few flowers is usually enough.

### Wall spaces

Large areas of undecorated wall space can look bleak. Pedestal arrangements of varying sizes are an ideal way to break up the space and depending upon the amount of space, your florist should be able to advise on pedestal sizes. Pedestals refer to any arrangement that is free-standing. Sometimes based on a metal wrought-iron pedestal, similar to those often found in churches, sometimes trompe l'oeil (meaning literally, fooling the eye), made from fibreglass to look like a classical marble column, the pedestal on which the flowers are arranged to give height can complement the style of room or the look you are trying to achieve in a marquee. Florists can usually hire in different pedestals according to the tastes of their clients. For weddings at home, pieces of furniture can do well in place of pedestals to raise flower arrangements off the ground and add an intimate, homely feel to the decoration. Almost anything will do – plant stands, bedside cabinets even. If you are worried about seeing the furniture and you do not like it, do not ignore the possibility offered by the draping and swagging

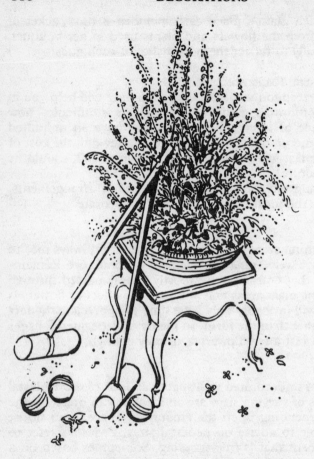

of fabric to disguise legs and worse. Polyester linings from
dressmaking suppliers are inexpensive to buy, even in quantity,
and imitate silk quite well enough for the purpose and come in
a dazzling range of colours.

*Table centres*
If you are having tables of any kind, you must think about
some sort of decoration to go in the centre of the tables. For
an informal reception at which the tables are more for what
is termed 'occasional' use, i.e. for glasses and ashtrays rather
than for eating at, the tables themselves will usually be quite

small and you will not have the space for anything very large. If guests are sitting down to eat, the tables will generally be larger and since the focus of the attention of the guests as they eat is towards the middle of the table, you need to give plenty of thought and allow a little more of the budget to what you put in the middle.

Table centres can be made from and with almost anything. Pretty rustic baskets which are always cheaper to buy in a flower market than from a retail outlet are an ideal way of hiding the oasis most florists will have to use to keep a supply of water to cut flowers. These rustic baskets fit country weddings very well and are sometimes made of dried foliage and scented plants, such as lavender or fennel and the smell from the baskets will support the flowers. Larger baskets can be used to contain arrangements for other areas. Try to remember to put something in the loos which are often forgotten and can be rather bleak.

Candelabra, either in wrought iron or silver can be decorated with flowers, fresh or sugar-frosted fruits, foliages and an infinite number and variety of other props, such as shells or strings of fake pearls. Candelabra give height to the centre of the tables, which can be very important in a large, cavernous space. Remember to be extremely careful about the use of

naked flame anywhere, especially in a marquee. Larger forms of table centre such as candelabra can obscure the line of vision of the guests and make conversation across a table difficult. In general, these forms of larger table centre are usually only used for larger tables, probably 6' in diameter, and it is actually quite difficult to have a conversation across such a large table anyway. It is a personal matter though and you should give some thought to this. To create interest and decoration and to literally populate the space in a large, high room or tent, tall flower arrangements do give an exciting effect with none of the problems associated with garlanding walls or trying to hang things from ceilings.

Anything used to decorate candelabra should be flame-proofed if it is likely to catch fire. Flame-retardant spray can be bought commercially and used to treat any fabric or decorative element you are planning to incorporate.

Detta Phillips is an extremely creative and talented florist, used to working with brides, and has put together some ideas for seasonal table centres you might like to think about.

---

SEASONAL TABLE CENTRES

*For Spring*

Country flowers, picked from the garden (if planted in October!). Very simple, pretty and feminine and arranged in chunky vases filled with stones, mossed baskets, terracotta pots or even milk jugs or jam jars. Overflowing apple and cherry blossoms, white lilac, catkins, deep purple and pink anemones, white parrot tulips, bluebells and hyacinths.

*For Summer*

To create height and interest, instead of a low arrangement for people to talk over, an arrangement for people to talk through. 3 foot tall, loosely rounded 'trees', standing in mossed terracotta pots. Cow parsley, beech, peonies, foxgloves, stocks, old fashioned roses and halved lemons. Entwined around the stem of the tree, honeysuckle and strings of strawberries, with more strawberries tumbling out and around the base.

*For Autumn*

For a harvest feeling, groups of terracotta pots arranged together and piled high with blackberries, crab apples, radishes and mushrooms, tumbling and spilling over on to a base of bark, moss, rosehips and old man's beard. Guests will enjoy eating any soft fruits!

*For Winter*

For a Christmas wedding, something rich, opulent and spicy. Baskets swathed in deep red/burgundy velvet and filled with shiny dark green foliage, such as camelia or rhododendron leaves, fully blown wine red and cream roses, clusters of sprayed gold walnuts, fir cones, tied bunches of cinnamon sticks and a thick church candle in the centre.

*Garlands, swags and arches*
Garlands, for tent poles and tables, are very popular. These can be extremely pretty, but very labour-intensive to put together and consequently expensive. If you would like to garland poles or columns, consult your florist as to the most cost-effective way of achieving the end result you want. If you know a keen gardener, there are, in fact, products on the market now which basically consist of a long polythene-enclosed sausage of potting soil which can be used to literally grow garlands of suitable plants such as lobelia or gypsophila. Because they are growing plants and you have a great deal of earth, they are more delicate and more difficult to attach than cut flowers made into a garland by a florist, but can be used to great effect outside, such as around a garden fence or the exterior archway of a church. This is an inexpensive solution and you can also watch the garland grow in the months leading up to the wedding. The same products are also available to create wreaths – just make sure that the plants used have very bridal connotations and avoid anything funereal.

Long top tables for the bridal party, often used in conjunction with round tables for the guests are ideal for decorating with garlands and swags and this can be done relatively inexpensively. Ivy, smilax and creepers of all kinds are the best foliages to create the basic structure, using flowers at intervals to create the colour and depth. Using creepers of any kind, particularly woody-stemmed ivies, it is essential that the cut end be thoroughly bashed and allowed to soak in water for at least two days before it is used. Otherwise even ivy which is cut on the morning of a wedding will wither and dry out long before the speeches.

Arches of flowers or foliage are beautiful, but again, because of the work they represent, they can be an expensive way of decorating an area. Ask your florist about ways you might achieve the effect, perhaps using some trellising they might have, or could hire in. Do not underestimate fabric for arches. Suitably swagged fabric between two very ordinary fence posts or larch poles driven into the ground can create an exciting and elegant frame for an entrance. It could be taken further with the addition of pretty bows, foliage or garlands of beads or artificial pearls.

*Colour*

Do not be afraid to introduce some colour to your wedding. Brides often think that it is only appropriate to stick to pastel shades or cream and white flowers for a wedding. These can be very bland. Foliage should always be used in a variety of greens to give depth, from the almost acid lemony-green to the very dark colours of laurel and ivy.

Another important point to remember about white flowers in particular is that they are often the most expensive. Lilies, roses, stocks, lily of the valley are all beautiful, fragrant and costly. Certain times of the year put the prices up even further. Keeping the cost of wedding flowers down does mean using what is in season and abundance. In spring, bulbs abound. Tulips, daffodils and all the delicious smelling narcissi are ideal for weddings. In summer, roses, rhododendrons, peonies, delphiniums are in season. In the autumn, the colours of turning leaves and foliages create a seasonal backdrop to the golds of sunflowers and hops or reddish or rust-coloured berries. Winter weddings, though a problem for many flowers out of season, yet have all the Christmas foliage and colours at their disposal. Do try to use the time of year to your own best advantage, to the best effect and in the most creative way you can.

FLOWERS FOR THE CEREMONY

*Register Office*
A civil wedding is a short ceremony, lasting on average 20–30 minutes. It would be impossible for a Registrar to allow every couple he or she marries to decorate the room in which the marriage is to take place in their own way, without chaos ensuing. No decoration is made to the office or room in which the marriage takes place, although most Registrars will have some sort of table arrangement.

A civil bride may, if she chooses, carry a bouquet, as may her attendants if she has any and it is normal for the male members of the party to wear buttonholes as they would for other types of weddings.

*Flowers for a civil ceremony in a licensed venue*
Unlike civil marriages in Register Offices, you may decorate your licensed venue to match the overall theme of your reception. The Registrar would be unlikely to object to your decoration provided you weren't planning any directly religious symbols made out of flowers!

*Church weddings and blessings*
Weddings in church are traditionally associated with flowers as are many other occasions in the church calendar – Easter, Harvest Festival, Christmas, for example. Customs for decorating churches for weddings differ around the world, but in general the principles are fairly straightforward. A wedding is a joyous occasion to celebrate and the appearance of the church should reflect this.

Before you make any decision on the type of decoration to the church, you must first consult the minister. Some ministers have very precise views on how far the decoration should be allowed to go and what sort of flowers are appropriate. Others will leave all this entirely up to you, but you must find out first. You may be asked to ensure that specific pedestals are used or that arrangements are or are not placed on altars and other areas.

A blessing is a service performed for a couple who have already been legally married. Blessings are performed within the various Protestant denominations and the content and style of the service varies considerably. In general, the decoration of a church for a blessing would follow the same lines as for a full wedding but would perhaps be a little simpler.

The areas normally decorated for weddings can be any of the following:

Entrances or gateways – often with arches of flowers;
Pew ends – may be decorated with small bunches of flowers, but remember if the aisle is narrow, these could get knocked off;
Window sills;
Small tables at the beginning of the aisle;
Pedestal arrangements at the end of the aisle;
The altar;
The font;
The pulpit;
Columns – with garlands or crowns of flowers.

It would be extremely expensive to try to tackle all these areas, so visit the church with friends as well as your florist and family to decide how best to achieve the effect.

At any time of the year, particular churches may be holding more than one wedding on the same day. This likelihood increases dramatically in the summer. If two or more couples are being married in the same church on the same day, it stands to reason that there will not be time for the flowers to be installed and removed for each different wedding. A wise minister will bring together the couples concerned to avoid any squabbling and also with a view to spreading the costs between the parties concerned. It is always worth checking during your initial prenuptial meeting how busy the church will be on your chosen day and indeed the days leading up to it. Remember too, that portable arrangements can be whisked from the church to the reception by a few ushers in the time it takes to have photographs outside the church, provided the minister has agreed to this.

*Synagogues*
The style in which you decorate a synagogue must be something you discuss with the Rabbi or Secretary. Like churches, synagogues differ greatly in style and layout and, like churches, they often have high echoing spaces. If money is limited, think in terms of two or three beautifully stocked arrangements at

focal points rather than a series of mean offerings. No decoration to the Ark should ever be considered without the Rabbi's approval.

The central focus for most Jewish brides is the chuppah underneath which the ceremony will take place. Chuppahs vary in style and age and will sometimes be very delicate, demanding care and attention to their decoration. If possible, a chuppah is usually heavily decorated with flowers, symbolising as it does, the home which the couple will now set up together.

## *Bridal flowers*

Most brides carry a bouquet of fresh flowers which can consist of a simple posy of country flowers or a wired bridal shower, or anything in between, according to taste. The cost of a bouquet is directly the result of who makes it, what flowers are chosen to go into it and how long it takes to put together. Bridal bouquets are steeped in tradition and the significance of including certain flowers in the content changes subtly over the centuries. The Victorians greatly favoured orange blossom and rosemary and Victorian brides would plant the cuttings of rosemary in their bouquet into their new gardens to supply the bridal bouquets of their own daughters.

Not all brides choose to carry bouquets. Some opt instead for bibles or prayer books and others decide against carrying anything at all. It is important to remember that young women used to carry flowers or used them to decorate their person on a much more general basis in the past, for everything from village fairs to funerals. Flowers have always been seen as a fashion accessory. As you arrive for your wedding, the first impression your guests have will be of you behind whatever you decide to carry and therefore the scale and choice of bouquet need to be chosen to fit the style of your dress. Big girls with tiny posies and little girls carrying large shrubs are a bit comical. Think about your bouquet as though it were a handbag to fit the scale of your outfit.

Few brides would not look ravishing with a little floral decoration here and there. There are few enough occasions in our lives when we can actually get away with turning up flower bedecked. A few single florets literally sprinkled into a hairstyle can be far more effective than a great crown of blooms. Inspiration for the use of flowers, as with wedding dresses, should be sought from old paintings. If you can spare the time to visit a local gallery and see how ladies of all ages used flowers to enhance their appearance rather than disguise it, you will probably find this a far more profitable exercise than simply consulting bridal magazines or florists.

*Headdresses and wreaths*

Anything floral worn on your head must be chosen with thought to the hairstyle you plan for the day. An extremely complicated coiffure, with pleats, fringes and ringlets does not need the addition of a large collection of flowers. Long loose hair is the perfect foil for indulging the wildest or even the simplest flights of floral fancy.

Headdresses of any kind, be they floral or not, present logistical problems if worn with a veil. Anything with spikes can easily catch the delicate fabric of a veil and pollen needs to be removed from any flowers likely to drop it.

*Attendants*

The clothing and accessories of bridesmaids and other attendants should be chosen to match or echo the bride's choice. Little children are not always good at carrying things very sensibly. Flower baskets are popular for little girls, as are decorated hoops and tiny posies. Little boys do look more dignified without flowers, but decorated drums can be fun. Adult bridesmaids look positively ridiculous unless a certain respect is shown to their age, and will normally carry a smaller, simplified version of the bride's choice of bouquet.

## Male members of the party and ushers

The groom, his best man, ushers and both his and the bride's father will normally wear a single flower perhaps with a little foliage, in the buttonhole of their jackets. It is not necessary to supply the entire congregation with buttonholes. If funds are very limited, there is an old Victorian custom you might revive, of tying a simple white ribbon in a bow through the buttonhole in place of a flower – unusual and very good for hay fever sufferers.

## Mothers and grandmothers

The mothers of the bride and groom may choose whether to wear a corsage of flowers, which is only slightly larger in content than a buttonhole. If this is the case, care must go into matching the corsage to the colour of the outfits and the flowers in general.

## Artificial flowers and plants

Put off by the high price and short lifespan of real flowers, some families do choose artificial decoration instead. There are two sorts of artificial flowers and plants – those which try to imitate life and those which do not.

With the best will in the world, artificial flowers and plants cannot look natural unless exceptionally good quality imitations are expertly used. The cheaper imitations which are more commonly used can result in a wedding marquee or reception room looking more like a cheap hotel somewhere at the far end of the Bayswater Road.

The other immediately significant point to make about artificial flowers is that they have no scent. There is something fresh about even unscented natural foliage. To counteract this problem, many suppliers of artificial flowers have introduced the practice of spraying them with imitation floral fragrances, which are sadly most often revolting. If you are intending to use artificial flowers, choose your own spray with care.

The best use of artificial flowers involves those which do not pretend to be real, and have the courage of their convictions as imitations. Crepe paper flowers from Mexico are ideal for this sort of thing and can be used to twist around tables, tent poles, fences and almost anything. These flowers are ideal for fiestas and fêtes and any celebration where space needs to be filled up with form and colour.

The conclusion must be that if you are trying to achieve a natural look, do all you can to afford real flowers, in minimal quantities with maximum foliage. If you want a more exotic look, or are prepared to use artificial flowers with creativity, go for those which do not pretend to be anything other than what they really are.

## 2. Using fabric and ribbons

Reference has already been made to some uses you might find for fabric to decorate your wedding. Stripy, spotted or tartan fabrics give an instant flash of colour and opulence and do not need to be expensive. Always use flame-retardant fabric or treat it yourself with the appropriate product.

For binding bouquets, around tent poles, for cake tables and top tables, along garden gates and fences, even carefully used in trees, spectacular effects can be achieved with fabric and ribbon. The best method of attaching fabric for decorative use is a staple gun, which can damage anything valuable; sellotape is a more gentle, if not quite so secure, alternative.

Ribbon can be bought in crushed paper, silk, satin, cotton velvet or organza, and is extremely versatile. It can also be bought wired at the edges to help bows keep their shape. It is always best to buy ribbon in large quantity from wholesalers as it is very easy to use up several metres in one go. Think about using several different complementary colours rather than just one.

## 3. Other props

There are a great number of 'props' which you can employ to fill empty corners of rooms or marquees. Furniture has already been mentioned, but croquet sets, gardening tools, planters and pots used as still lifes, or even a bale of hay tied up with a tartan ribbon, can have an amusing and dramatic effect. Whatever the setting of your wedding, you will be able to think of elements to give lightness, humour and a creative personal touch.

How far themes should be pursued is a personal decision to be made. Themes can be loosely based on colour or take the geographical setting or time of year. They can also follow a historical angle or be inspired by the choice of food served at the reception.

## COLOUR AS A THEME

Colour is the most obvious theme you can introduce to a wedding. Colours as themes are normally translated into the flowers used and other decorative elements, but should be chosen to suit people, since a colour theme will often be followed through into the clothing of the bride, groom and their attendants. Certain colours can be hard for some people to wear.

## HISTORY AS A THEME

Some settings for weddings offer an immediate and strong historical theme for a bride. An ancient chapel or a castle as a reception venue give instant force to a medieval style wedding dress. One should never feel obliged to follow a theme just for the sake of it, but a strong theme should never conflict with its setting.

## GEOGRAPHY AS A THEME

A country wedding is a country wedding and should be respected as such. A bride should not turn up in a city suit. A town wedding is a town wedding and a little more sophistication should be aspired to. Bridal parties which emerge on to busy Saturday shopping streets, led by armies of flower fairies looking as though they should be skipping about fields rather than dodging the traffic on the A3, can be a most bizarre sight.

Weddings in Scotland beg the use of tartan and heather and a few carefully chosen thistles, drams of whisky after dinner and the odd highland fling. Kentish weddings would not be the same without a few hops thrown in for good measure and some good local cider on offer. Never be afraid to include regional specialities as dishes on the menu or as part of the liquid refreshment.

Every bride should be encouraged to use the setting of her wedding and reception to her best advantage. If you can walk to the church, or lead your guests back from it in procession, down little country lanes, then do so. If avoiding busy weekend traffic of old ladies, prams and tourists means leaving the church instantly without photographs, consider doing so. Avoid the incongruous and you avoid the ridiculous.

## 4. Balloons

People either love balloons or they hate them. Used well, balloons can be an ideal form of decoration for any party, including a wedding. Balloon manufacturers and suppliers have been quick to understand the specific preferences of some brides and a whole range of wedding balloons is now available, confetti-filled, heart-shaped, latex or metal, air- or helium-filled, crystal-clear bubbles to black with silver stars.

Balloons used by professional suppliers bear little resemblance to those from our childhood parties. They are infinitely more sophisticated both in appearance and potential and balloon installation and theming is quite a trade in itself. Breathtaking arrangements of arches and tunnels, roofs over dance floors, columns and sculptures can be made from balloons.

Balloons supplied by a professional, though often inexpensive compared to equivalent quantities of real flowers, are not cheap. The price of the actual balloons themselves is not the significant cost. It is the labour time involved and the transportation of the balloons which together provide the price, so you will need to be sure that any quotation provided for balloons is all-inclusive.

# CHAPTER 8
# Entertainment

## 1. Reception music

It is important to remember that in any religion or culture, weddings have always been a cause for celebration. Once the ceremony is over, the time has come for fun. Wedding reception music does not need to be solemn or particularly formal.

Choosing the sort of music which will be best for your reception is one of the many chain reaction decisions you will need to make once you have decided on your wedding format. It also needs to be considered in the light of the style of the reception venue.

### CLASSICAL MUSIC

Musicians who play classical instruments are usually highly trained and, being professionals, they can normally adapt to play solo or in duos, trios or quartets. Classical musicians will not normally choose to play with amplification which can so easily distort the clarity of the sound produced, so it is important to have a group of musicians of a size appropriate to acoustics and the number and noise of guests.

## JAZZ

Jazz covers a variety of different styles. Some jazz bands look so bizarre that if it was not for the excellent quality of their music and comic timing, you might be forgiven for thinking they were buskers. Others echo the big bands of the 1920s and 1930s in sharp suits and slicked back hair. You should never discount the effect the appearance as well as the sound of a band can have upon the behaviour of your guests. Using a madcap band of buskers at a formal evening dance would be as wrong as using a sophisticated 1920s style trio for a barn dance. Music must be planned to match the style of everything else.

## MODERN

There are plenty of professional groups of musicians who specialise in performing well-known songs as entertainment for parties of all kinds. To be sure to get the right band for you, make your choice from the widest possible selection and compare styles and prices.

## MUSICAL AGENCIES

There are a number of agencies which specialise in providing musicians for weddings and other parties. You should not be put off by the thought that you will almost certainly be paying a fee of some sort for the privilege of having it all arranged for you. Any good, professional agency will doubtless be better at finding exactly what it is you want and will insist on a level of competence from the band you may not be able to guarantee in any other way.

Regardless of whether you are approaching a musician or a band directly or using the services of an agency, always:

1. Ask for demonstration cassettes and if possible videos so that you get a good idea of what they look and sound like.
2. Ensure that the price you accept is inclusive of VAT, transportation and any other expenses you might incur.
3. Check how long the fee quoted will actually cover. Most bands will perform two or more sets of about 40 minutes.

Musicians do need breaks every now and again and you will want to plan the timing of the reception so that the breaks coincide with when you need silence for speeches, or meals. Try to avoid losing momentum.

4. Ask whether you are expected to provide food and drink for the band. Your caterer will need to know and you will need to plan for this expense.

5. Make sure the band have maps and good directions to find you and know where and if they can park and exactly what time you would like them to arrive and start to play. They may need a room in which to change, or leave their personal effects securely.

6. Find out if the band is due to perform anywhere where you might pop along to see them in action before you pay a deposit to confirm a booking.

7. Check amplification requirements, particularly in marquees. If the band needs electricity, you will be expected to have provided it. Not all bands have their own PA equipment, so remember to ask.

8. Discuss the play list. If you have particular favourite songs, they could be included. Do the musicians know what song you would like to have played to start off the dancing?

## 2. Evening dances and discotheques

One major advantage of a discotheque over a live band is that a disc jockey can provide non-stop music if required to do so, in a variety of different musical styles over the course of the evening, whereas even an energetic band requires the odd break. Breaks, however well timed, can mean that some atmosphere is lost and it can be hard to get guests dancing again. The ideal balance for an evening party is to have both so that the discotheque can take over before, during breaks, and after the band stops playing. If it comes to a choice of one or the other, a discotheque could well win.

There is always an advantage to having a fairly broad mix of musical styles played during a dance to encourage people of all ages on to the dance floor. Finding the right discotheque operator needs the same careful and attentive investigation as a band and the same rules ALWAYS apply. Some operators offer a simple musical service with the odd flashing coloured bulb, others install a mini nightclub with superb light displays, lasers and smoke machines and there is

naturally a huge discrepancy in price. Sophisticated discotheques can be very expensive indeed and it would be silly to
plan an evening party without giving proper attention to how
much the music could cost. If you are unable to afford good
music, do not plan a dance.

Working out a play list is in many ways even more important
if using a discotheque rather than a band. Arrange an evening
with some friends and ask for their suggestions for all those
songs you used to dance to together. You will find this an
amusing way of spending an evening.

Here is the advice of Frank Hughes, who, for many years,
has organised music for weddings:

---

FRANK HUGHES

Music plays a significant role in the daily life of every individual
from earliest childhood and for a musician it gives the greatest
joy to see the pleasure a particular piece of music can bring to
a guest or couple at a wedding ceremony or reception.

A certain piece of music can recall a happy occasion, a
meeting, mood or period of one's life and can, conversely,
create a special place in the senses which can be re-created for
that person or couple time and time again by the merest aural
'glimpse' of the music.

The musical side of weddings and receptions is often given
least attention. There is an overwhelming choice of groups of
musicians on the market and many of these musicians give
little thought to the task in hand other than playing the
instruments and music that they know and which they play in
a rather introverted manner, often with little thought to
presentation.

Many prospective brides, grooms and parents are embarrassed when initially discussing musical requirements. They
may know and love many pieces of music, whether classical or
popular, but often cannot remember the titles or names of
composers and it is important to offer as much information as
possible, even to hum a tune. It is the aim of a sensitive music
consultant or performer to ease a client through these minor
difficulties without any intimidation or snobbishness and to
play the favourite music in the best shape or form.

There now exists a variety of recorded music suitable for ceremonies and receptions and this can be purchased in most good record shops. These CDs or tapes are an ideal guide if there is no initial preference and I would advise any client to seek out such guidelines in the first instance. Given the resources and instruments, any piece of music can be arranged, performed and sung at any point during the wedding day.

As a music consultant, the first contact with the client will involve listening to any suggestions and assimilating information given for each aspect of the wedding. Help can be freely given regarding taste and style of music and suggestions as to the most useful and economic ensemble which could perform, perhaps both at the ceremony and the reception. A string quartet of two violins, viola and 'cello, the performers dressed in white tie and tails, can play at the church, accompany the congregation with organ and choir for the hymns, perform dignified music as the guests arrive and during the signing of the register and even accompany a soprano soloist in a favourite piece of sacred music such as 'Ave Maria'. Anthems performed by the church choir can also be accompanied by the quartet. Given a discreet exit, the musicians can proceed to the reception and be ready to greet the wedding party with joyous classical music and adapt to the ebullient mood with many lighter popular arrangements of Scott Joplin, Gershwin, Cole Porter, Lennon-McCartney, etc.

However, should you want dancing at your wedding, you might consider a trio of keyboard (or piano, which can be hired), saxophone and drums, or similar. Most of these function musicians double as singers and have their own comprehensive quality PA equipment which can be assembled with the minimum of fuss and is included in their fees. A microphone can be supplied for speeches, announcements and the like. A good function trio will cover all styles of background and dance music and carry a wide variety of taped background music for short breaks. Styles include old-time dancing, waltzes, foxtrots, quicksteps, tangos, etc. They can perform modern pop and rock and roll with the addition of instruments such as guitar, Latin percussion and extra keyboards. The band can create a Brazilian samba feel with Latin percussion and a female singer. Country and Western music and square-dance, barn-dance, blues and soul music are all part of the 'staple diet' of every competent band-player. A larger dance band with a brass and rhythm section and singers can play Glenn Miller and 20s to 40s Big Band favourites and still adapt to more modern sounds. It should be the aim of good musicians and band-leaders to follow the mood of the event and if necessary change the style of music played to fit the atmosphere.

One of the most important points to remember is that on no other occasion will one encounter such a wide variety of ages, family and friends from different backgrounds. Every guest will have a personal preference in music and as much as the bride, groom and their families may have specific ideas as to what they would like to hear or dance to, it is equally important to create something which can and will give pleasure to all present and which they will remember with great affection. While a good function band will entertain the younger set, teenagers will often feel that they lack the real contemporary disco sounds and sheer volume levels they crave, and the provision of a disco with a first-class D.J. in a room away from the band is always a good idea. Of course, if the reception takes place in a marquee, the band and disco can alternate.

Of all the groups that can be engaged, perhaps one of the most popular is the trio of violin, accordion and double bass. The acoustic nature of this ensemble enables them to play 'al fresco' (given a suitable climate!), to be completely mobile, and still be able to connect up to a small and discreet amplification inside on a stage or floor space, to be heard by a larger party. With the addition of guitar, a singer, drums, saxophone, etc. this can be very successful for dancing. This would be a very versatile band, able to adapt to almost any style of music allowing the bride and groom to plan a nicely diverse programme.

Each group will do its best to include personal favourites of any type of music that suits the line-up and a list of requests will be welcomed by a good band-leader before the reception. Nowadays it is possible to cater for most international types of music and dance with a choice of continental, Asian, African, Middle and Far Eastern and South American bands for back-ground music and dancing.

It is important to realise that every musician needs reasonable rest periods in a comfortable and quiet environment, adequate food and drink when required, at a time convenient for caterers and given this, they will be able to perform to the very best of their abilities. A good banqueting manager, master of ceremonies or toast-master will liaise in these matters and advise musicians when to play specific music for the entrance of the bride and groom, during the cake cutting and departure.

Prospective brides and grooms who expect the party to dance the night away till dawn should remember that there are few who can last longer than a day of travel, excitement, food and drink, dancing and conversation. A good option would be to engage the band for a nominal period with the option of overtime priced, pro-rata, in hourly or half-hourly units. Overtime after midnight is usually charged at double the normal rate and this is an area you should be careful not to commit yourself to unnecessarily.

Finally, don't forget that the musicians have to remove instruments, drums and PA equipment which can be done deftly and discreetly, but if a delay is necessary due to continuation of the party, speeches, etc., extra cost can be involved.

It only remains to be said that it is the aim of every truly professional musician and entertainer to make every wedding the most personal and memorable for their audience and for the best consultant or adviser to guide their client to this goal.

## 3. Other entertainment

Though not by any means traditional at a wedding, there are plenty of forms of entertainment other than musical, which when used in the right situation and at the right time can greatly add to the enjoyment of your guests.

Close-up magicians will wander among the guests, performing astounding magic tricks to small groups with well-practised comic timing.

Caricature cartoonists will wander similarly, presenting guests prepared to sit for them with a personal portrait.

Cabaret artists of a wide variety can be booked to perform all sorts of shows from juggling to comedy or mime.

William Bartholomew is well known for getting the music

just right at weddings. Here, he gives us some good pointers:

---

WILLIAM BARTHOLOMEW ENTERTAINMENTS

One of the most important ingredients of any wedding or wedding reception is the music.

It is always worth calling a professional for help and advice if you are booking a choir, organist, string quartet or band, and it can be a good idea to telephone your local music college who can provide first-class musicians at a very reasonable rate. However when it comes to good dance bands, discotheques or cabaret acts then a party organiser can be very helpful and full of unusual ideas, and generally they will offer the right entertainment for the 'job'.

It is well worth spending a little bit more on the music as guests always remember a good band and they certainly remember a bad one.

Volume is another factor and it is important that your band or discotheque do not interfere with guests' conversation. A meeting with the band leader or disc jockey should eliminate any fears and a helpful discussion about music is also important.

Unusual cabaret acts such as mime artists, graphologists, magicians and circus acts can also be fun and they will make the party a little bit more memorable.

Remember, by using an organiser or entertainments company will ensure the smooth running of your wedding reception leaving you free to enjoy the day to the full!

---

Fireworks are popular for all sorts of parties. Professional firework companies can arrange for displays to suit all budgets from a single enormous rocket let off into the night sky as a couple leave their reception, to a display coordinated with music lasting as long as a budget can manage. If you would like to have fireworks at your wedding, you will need to consider who or what is likely to be disturbed by them. Farmers do have an understandable tendency to become irate if livestock are disturbed and elderly neighbours will be justified in making a complaint if not warned in advance.

CHILDREN

If you know that there will be more than a handful of children at your wedding reception, you might like to give some consideration as to how to keep them occupied and under control. Never underestimate the destructive capacity of a bored toddler.

Some brides decide that the only way round this problem is to ban children from their weddings. For any parent, this can pose a serious problem in that it is not always easy or suitable to find babysitters and they may well feel that they are unable to attend the wedding as a result of this ultimatum.

Lovely and sweet though they are, the threat of unruly children must be addressed. A useful idea for any bride would be to place a table for the children in the corner of the room or marquee, full of healthy children-style food, colouring books, games and a few toys. If warned in advance, caterers will be able to provide a friendly member of staff to be responsible for supervising and entertaining the children. Bouncy castles and children's entertainers will also always go down well, not necessarily just with the under-fives.

Finally, on the subject of children, you must give thought to their safety. If there is a pond, stream, swimming pool or river anywhere near the reception venue, it is logical that at least one small person will find it. The best outcome is that they return muddy and wet. The worst is that they do not return at all. Children are desperately vulnerable. Busy roads, poisonous plants, marquee ropes and animals do pose a real threat. Do not allow your wedding to have tragic consequences.

## 4. Music for the ceremony

Wedding services held in churches and synagogues will usually include musical elements. It is very much a personal decision whether to build upon the existing music in the form of hymns or psalms sung by introducing pieces for choirs or soloists to sing or organists or musicians to play. According to the religion or denomination in question, certain restrictions may be imposed to ensure that any music is in keeping with the solemnity of the occasion. At the very least, a bride is normally expected to contribute to her wedding ceremony by making a choice of music with which to enter the church or synagogue with her father and with which to leave in triumphant procession with her husband. She and the groom will usually choose the hymns and readings for a church wedding, although according to the officiating minister's personal views, this choice is not necessarily open-ended. The same guidance is likely to apply to Jewish weddings.

It is important to consult the minister who will marry you before coming to any firm decisions on music. If you would like to have the presence of a choir at your wedding and there is no regular choir, the minister may well be able to help you find one at a reasonable cost. The same will apply to soloists and even musicians. If not, you will have to look further afield, but it is always polite and courteous to consult and to have your intentions approved before you waste time and effort pursuing what will not be regarded as suitable or advisable.

## 5. Music for a civil ceremony

Many couples planning a civil marriage do not realise that they are entitled to add music and readings to the ceremony whether this is to take place in a venue licensed for civil marriages or even in a Register Office. Weddings in Register Offices no longer need to be seen as the less interesting option and couples can now tailor the ceremony to make it personal and appropriate. The actual choices of music and readings are at the discretion of the Registrar and must be approved by him/her well in advance of the wedding. Words and music written for religious devotion in any context are not acceptable, nor are those which have commonly been used for weddings. For example, Wagner's Bridal March from *Lohengrin* ('Here Comes the Bride') would not be permitted. The best idea is to submit a potential list.

# The Next Step

# CHAPTER 1
# Printing

Once you know what sort of reception you are going to have, where it will be and have confirmed the date and time of the ceremony, it is time to start thinking about invitations.

Forty years ago, wedding invitations were usually sent out no more than three to four weeks in advance of the wedding. Most modern brides would probably be shocked to learn this. How could you possibly plan for numbers? How could your guests plan to attend with so little notice? When would you have time to consider table and seating plans?

Forty years ago, life was very different. Far fewer women were in full-time employment. Foreign travel was much less common. Europe was still suffering the repercussions of rationing from the Second World War and life in general had a slower and more predictable pace, weddings taking their place in the general scheme of things. This is a very good example of why wedding etiquette has had to change to suit the times in which people live.

Nowadays, wedding invitations are normally sent out 8–12 weeks in advance of the wedding. Three months is quite long enough for guests to make arrangements to attend your wedding. The only exception to this would be for a wedding taking place abroad, where it is in your interests to give guests good warning of the extra cost and travel involved.

Even allowing three months for guests to book local accommodation may not be enough. Hotels can become booked up early by touring parties and foreign visitors. Rather than sending your invitations out too early, why not make provisional bookings at local hotels and guest houses, explaining that these are for your wedding, and including information on what has been provisionally booked when you do send your invitations, along with the other information you must enclose such as maps and directions to the various venues in question? This means that when guests do receive their invitations, they can simply contact the hotel of their choice and confirm the booking directly themselves. Always try to give a reasonable variety of accommodation in your choice to suit all budgets.

## 1. Compiling the invitation list

Both families should be involved in the drawing up of the list and, as far as possible, guests should be chosen to provide a good representation of the friends and families of both the bride and groom. It is easier to cross someone off a list than to find that they have been forgotten.

The established number of guests must be approved by whoever is paying the costs of the wedding to avoid antagonism. The number of guests will determine how many invitations you need to order. You will probably not need equal numbers for the simple reason that many invitations will be double or joint although you must allow for making mistakes while writing guests' names and addresses. You should also think about having invitations to send to important people in your life who you know already cannot come. It is a thoughtful gesture to send them an invitation anyway. If you do receive a large number of refusals, there is nothing to prevent you from sending a second wave of invitations, provided that you have not left this insultingly late and thereby make it obvious to the recipient that they were not an immediate choice.

The printing, writing and addressing of invitations can take some time and should never be rushed. Even if you are not planning to send your invitations out for a while, provided you have all the information you need, there is nothing to stop you from having them printed. Always try to avoid the last minute scribbling of envelopes in nasty biro. Use a nice black pen and give yourself time to enjoy even this administrative process.

As you write your invitations, you will probably find that you have to depend upon members of your families to supply the full names and addresses of many of your guests. To avoid having to go through the compilation process a second time and expensive telephone calls to your parents after the wedding, keep this list safe. You will need it again in order to send thank you letters for the presents you will certainly receive. It is a good idea to make yourself a little form, as a 'Guest management record', which you will keep as the central information point. You can give yourself columns for information such as whether or not a guest has replied, if they are coming, what present they have sent, whether they have been thanked for it, whether they require special food, what table number they are to be placed at.

Being strictly correct, the envelope of a wedding invitation sent to a married couple is addressed to the wife only. The same 'rule' applies to invitations to any private social event, although the names of both of the couple – 'Mr and Mrs Jason Green' appear on the actual invitation. The only possible logic to be found in this little point of etiquette must be that for so many years, the wife has been the domestic and social secretary for the couple and therefore all diary dates would have been her traditional responsibility. How relevant this tradition remains today must be seen as a matter of personal choice.

Somewhat strangely, it has never been considered well mannered to send thank you letters to the hosts of a wedding, presumably for the simple reason that a bride's mother for example may feel duty bound to reply to a thank you letter and she is generally considered to have done enough already. In contrast to this argument, I personally consider that few brides' mothers would not be delighted to receive a letter of thanks once all the excitement is over and gone. It must be very nice to know that effort and expense have been so well received by guests and such a gesture could only be considered touching. Anyone genuinely wishing to send a letter of thanks, but worried that they might be breaching some ancient etiquette law might like to start off by saying something like, 'I know it is not really usual to write to the bride's parents after the wedding, but I simply had to send a little note to let you know what a lovely day it was. . .'

INVITATION STYLES

Wedding invitations can come in a variety of styles, from the very traditional to the very modern or individual. Traditional invitations would suggest that the wedding will be quite traditional. Extraordinary invitations would suggest a rather different sort of wedding.

## Hand-engraved invitations

The traditional wedding invitation consists of slightly raised, black script which is printed from a hand-engraved copperplate on to a folded sheet of good quality white or cream card, measuring anywhere between 7" × 4.5" to 8" × 6". This form of printing adheres to the traditions of diplomatic and Royal entertaining. Because the engraver must do his work in reverse, or negative, and the process is long and demands a great deal of skill, engraved invitations are more expensive than others. One particularly nice thing about having them, however, is that you will probably be given the actual copperplate from which the invitations were printed as a keepsake.

## Thermographed invitations

These are a good alternative to engraved invitations in that they mimic the style using a process called thermography. The invitations are printed and then subjected to a heating process during which the ink expands, thereby raising the script in imitation of the effect of copperplate printing. The end result is one which resembles the traditional form closely enough to fool most people. You do lose the subtlety and creativity of engraved invitations but you win in terms of speed and cost.

## Alternatives

There are many companies which specialise in 'Wedding Stationery', which usually incorporates certain romantic or topical elements into the design. Only you will know whether this sort of thing appeals to you. It is not really correct to send heavily embellished invitations to a wedding and weddings are quite romantic enough without needing the message enforced by the appearance of silver bells and pink hearts.

You could, however, think about approaching specific printers or graphic designers to produce something very personal and unique to match the approach you have taken to the wedding.

CHOOSING A PRINTER

Printers will have their own specialities and not all will be able to offer you as wide a range of printing styles as you might like. Before approaching any printer you should have a fairly good idea of the style of invitation you would like to send and of course how many you need so that they are able to supply an accurate quotation. You will need to know whether the price is inclusive of VAT, delivery or postage and any other charges to be incurred. You could discuss ink or paper colours, textures of card and any number of variable options open to you.

Printers will usually supply either a typeset layout or a proof for you to check and this is something you must take seriously or pay the consequences. Once the printing process is under way, it is expensive to rectify mistakes and can also cause unnecessary delay.

Before placing your invitation order anywhere, it is a good idea to think about other printing you might need in connection with the wedding. Prices are always better if a printer knows he is going to get a good deal of work from one client. You might need to think about a service sheet for a church wedding, or having a special cover printed for the 'Grace after Meals' booklet for a Jewish wedding. Menu cards could be chosen and you will certainly need some sort of stationery on which to write your thank you letters. This would be a good opportunity to have some personal stationery printed.

*Wording the invitations*

Invitations are always drafted in the third person. This means that they refer to the host using their full name and title. Wedding invitations are sent in the name of the hosts of the reception, in most cases the bride's parents. In some countries, the names of both sets of parents and sometimes grandparents appear on the invitation, so if you are marrying someone from a different country, you would be wise to check their traditions to avoid giving offence where none is intended.

If your reception is to take place at the home of a friend or relative, you might like to think about including their name on the invitation. While no fixed precedent exists, if the reception is to take place at the home of the parents of the groom it would be tactful to ask whether they would like their names included.

# THE TRADITIONAL
# WEDDING INVITATION

(Name of guest(s) written by hand
in top left-hand corner, using full
title 'Mr and Mrs John Smith')

*Mr and Mrs Alexander Taylor*
*request the pleasure of*
*your company at the marriage*
*of their daughter*
*Lucy*
*to*
*Mr Matthew Sharp*
*at St John's Church, Hampstead*
*on Saturday 20th June 1997*
*at 2 o'clock*
*and afterwards at*
*Heath House*

*R.S.V.P.*
*Heath House*
*Hampstead*
*London NW3 5QS*

# THE ALTERNATIVE
# TRADITIONAL FORM

*Mr and Mrs Alexander Taylor*
*request the pleasure*
*of the company of*

## (name of guest(s) filled in by hand)

......................................................................................

*at the marriage of their daughter*
*Lucy*
*to*
*Mr Matthew Sharp*
*at St John's Church, Hampstead*
*on Saturday 20th June 1997*
*at 2 o'clock*
*and afterwards at*
*Heath House*

*R.S.V.P.*
*Heath House*
*Hampstead*
*London NW3 5QS*

Brides and grooms whose parents are divorced, separated, remarried or widowed often panic at the idea of wording the invitation and there is really no need. The importance of the wording is to make clear the relationship of the individuals mentioned. In the case of divorced parents, it is difficult to set down hard and fast rules, as much will depend on who has brought the child up. If the bride lives with or has normally lived with her mother, the invitation will normally come from

her, with or without a second husband. The same applies to
the father of the bride. Whatever their current marital status,
divorced parents will often decide to host the reception
together anyway.


Bride's parents separated/divorced, but still sharing surname:


*Mr Alexander Taylor*

*and*

*Mrs Diana Taylor*

*request the pleasure of*

*your company at the marriage*

*of their daughter*

*Lucy*

*etc.*


Bride's parents divorced, mother remarried, hosting reception
together:


*Mr Alexander Taylor*

*and*

*Mrs Victor Green*

*request the pleasure of*

*your company at the marriage*

*of their daughter*

*Lucy*

*etc.*

Bride's parents divorced, mother absent or deceased, father remarried:

*Mr and Mrs Alexander Taylor*
*request the pleasure of*
*your company at the marriage*
*of his daughter*
*Lucy*
etc.

Bride's father absent or deceased, mother remarried:

*Mr and Mrs Victor Green*
*request the pleasure of*
*your company at the marriage*
*of her daughter*
*Lucy*                          (Taylor can be
etc.                     added if so desired)

Bride's mother widowed, not remarried:

*Mrs Alexander Taylor*
*requests the pleasure of*
*your company at the marriage*               .
*of her daughter*
*Lucy*
etc.

If the bride's parents are deceased, the reception may be hosted by a relative or friend:

*Mr and Mrs David Taylor*
*request the pleasure of*
*your company at the marriage*
*of his sister*
*Lucy*
*etc.*

If the bride is hosting the reception herself:

*Miss Lucy Taylor*
*requests the pleasure of*
*your company at her marriage*
*to*
*Mr Matthew Sharp*
*etc.*

Invitations may be sent without the name of a host:

*The pleasure of your company*
*is requested at the marriage of*
*Miss Lucy Taylor*
*and*
*Mr Matthew Sharp*
*etc.*

Invitations may be sent to a reception following a marriage which will already have taken place:

*Mr and Mrs Alexander Taylor*
*request the pleasure of*
*your company at a reception*
*following the marriage*
*of their daughter*
*Lucy*
*to*
*Mr Matthew Sharp*
*at Heath House, Hampstead*
*on Saturday 20th June 1997*
*at 6 o'clock*

Invitations may be sent to a Service of Blessing:

*Mr and Mrs Alexander Taylor*
*request the pleasure of your company*
*at the Blessing of the marriage*
*of their daughter*
*Lucy*
*etc.*

Or to a Register Office marriage:

*Lucy Taylor*

*and*

*Matthew Sharp*

*request the pleasure of your company*

*at their marriage*

*at Chelsea Register Office*

*on Friday, 23rd April 1997*

*at 11 o'clock*

*and afterwards for luncheon*

*etc.*

In addition, invitations may be sent to an evening party following the reception in which case they are usually printed on a single card and enclosed in the main invitation. They would normally be printed in 'landscape' rather than 'portrait' and would make a reference to whatever is planned: 'Dancing', 'Buffet', 'Dinner 9 o'clock', which would be printed in the bottom right hand corner as follows:

*Mr and Mrs Alexander Taylor*
*request the pleasure of your company*
*at an evening party to celebrate the marriage*
*of their daughter*
*Lucy*

*to*

*Mr Matthew Sharp*
*at Heath House, Hampstead*
*on Saturday 29th June 1997*
*at 8 o'clock*

*R.S.V.P.*                                                          *Black Tie*
*Heath House*                                          *Dinner and dancing*
*Hampstead*

Or to a civil wedding taking place in a licensed venue.

Since the change in the law governing marriages in the UK has only relatively recently permitted the solemnisation of civil marriages in venues other than Register Offices, there is no established etiquette in the wording of these invitations. The sensible thing is to choose whatever wording seems logical and informative. They might read:

*Mr and Mrs Alexander Taylor*
*request the pleasure of your company*
*at the marriage of their daughter*
*Lucy*
*to*
*Mr Matthew Sharp*
*at 30 Pavilion Road, London SW1*
*on Saturday 20th June 1997*
*at 11 o'clock*
*followed by a Reception*

Since there is no established precedent in the wording of an invitation to a civil marriage in a licensed venue, these offer a good opportunity to include a little more information perhaps than the traditionally worded invitation and you might in fact tell your guests that the marriage is:

*followed by Lunch(eon)/Dinner*

*Dress codes*
It is not correct to refer to morning dress on an invitation. For an evening celebration, it is correct to include 'Black Tie' if you wish your guests to wear evening dress.

THE CORRECT TRADITIONAL REPLY TO A WEDDING INVITATION
This letter should be handwritten, on headed paper, or with the address written at the top. The writing is centred on the page. The date appears at the bottom of the letter. Like the invitation, the letter is worded in the third person.

> *2, The Mansions*
> *Petersfield*
> *Surrey KY1 2PR*
>
> Miss Jane Green thanks Mr and Mrs Thomas Wright for
> their kind invitation to the marriage of their daughter
> Frances to Mr Justin French at the Church of St John, on
> Saturday 1st October 1997, and afterwards at The
> Clarendon Hotel, and has pleasure in accepting/but
> regrets that she is unable to attend.
>
> 12.7.97

## Reply cards

In the United Kingdom, there is no traditional precedent for
the use of reply cards. These are much more of a continental
custom, and popular in the United States. They do, however,
serve a purpose and it must be accepted that in certain
situations they make more logical sense than expecting guests
to reply in the formal way. Reply cards are usually pre-printed,
single cards with the date of the wedding and 'we can/cannot
attend' 'name(s)' options to be ticked and filled in. . . They
would normally also be enclosed in little envelopes which
would again be pre-printed with the host's address to ease their
being promptly sent back. Sending reply cards may mean that
guests do reply more promptly.

## Jewish wedding invitations

These are slightly different from the traditional wedding invitation in that a special line of Hebrew is often printed at the
very top of the invitation before the wording starts. Sometimes
the first names of both of the parents of the bride and groom
are printed, with the surname (rather than Mr and Mrs) and
reference to the groom is normally followed by 'son of' and
then the names of both of his parents. Otherwise these are
worded similarly.

If in any doubt, consult your printer for help and advice. He
will usually be very experienced.

## Place cards

Any seating plan for a meal will require place cards to show
guests where they are supposed to sit. These can be bought

commercially from any stationer, or printed personally for you, perhaps with your initials or other design included.

It is nice if you can consider the element of continuity in your choice of script styles and paper colours for the printing you arrange for your wedding. This does not mean that everything must match in a contrived way, but too many conflicting styles can look a little disorganised.

## Calligraphers

These are professional hand-writers and they can be booked to write invitations, place cards and seating plans and address envelopes and any other form of writing you might need for the wedding. Styles and prices vary, but in general they tend to charge on an hourly basis. You will need to give them plenty of time, because it is a labour-intensive process, but the end result can be breathtaking. Again, make sure you know in broad terms what you are committing yourself to financially before accepting an hourly rate.

## Service sheets

Service sheets are often printed for church weddings and blessings. These take the form of a piece of folded card, with or without a paper insert. The cover of the service sheet will have the names of the bride and groom printed in the bottom left and right hand corners respectively and the date and name of the church in which the service is to take place will be centred in the middle of the page. The actual layout of the service sheet will depend on the style of the ceremony and couples should seek advice from their minister before making firm arrangements for having service sheets printed.

## Menus

Even if you are planning to have a seated meal at your reception, you are not obliged to provide menu cards for your guests and this should be a budget decision, as they can be expensive, like anything else. Your hotel or reception venue may be able to provide these for you at a very low cost and this could be worth investigating.

## Postponed or cancelled marriages

If, for whatever reason, a wedding is cancelled after invitations have been sent out, the host/family will need to send a letter to all guests who have received an invitation. This letter would be worded in the third person:

'Mr and Mrs Alexander Taylor announce that the marriage of their daughter, Lucy, to Mr Matthew Green, which was arranged on 20th June 1997, will not now take place.'

If the wedding is merely postponed, new invitations will be sent out when a new date is fixed. If a new date has already been fixed when notification of the postponement is sent out, this will be mentioned in the letter, thereby avoiding the need for another set of invitations.

It would be acceptable, and certainly save the bride any embarrassment, for the reason for the postponement rather than the cancellation of the wedding to be briefly mentioned:

'Owing to the illness of Mrs Peter Smith, Mr and Mrs Alexander Taylor regret that they are obliged to postpone the invitations to the marriage of. . . '

The Wren Press is extremely experienced in dealing with the printing requirements of today's brides and grooms. Here are some thoughts from them:

---

WEDDING INVITATIONS

Wedding invitations are traditionally hand-engraved on folded white card.

The reasons for using engraving as a process used to be that it was simply the best method available of achieving a crisp and delicate fine line. For generations there was no other process which was comparable for clarity and delicacy. This is less true nowadays as technical advances in other methods of printing have reduced the quality gap. However, there is nothing that truly says top quality as clearly as a well-engraved copperplate invitation.

The other processes available for invitations are flat printing or thermography. A quick description of each process and its advantages and disadvantages might help the reader decide which process suits best.

*Flat printing*

This is potentially the most economical process and probably best suited to a design of an invitation which does not follow traditional lines. There is no limit to the scope and complexity of the possible design. Invitations vary from the simple paragraph of traditionally worded text to very much more exotic affairs.

## Thermography

In this process the printed image on the card is dusted with resin-based powder which, with the use of an extra heat process, forms a raised image. The attraction of this process is that an invitation can be produced within a few days, which looks similar in appearance to an engraved copperplate invitation but at a reduced cost.

## Engraved copperplate

The Rolls-Royce of invitations. An engraver uses a pointed and very sharp tool called a graver to engrave the text of the invitation on to a copperplate. It should be noted that what appears on the finished invitation is in effect an exact reproduction of the engraver's handwriting, with all that that implies in terms of inconsistencies and variations in the shape of characters – each plate should be considered a work of art. There are probably fewer than twenty-five engravers in Britain capable of engraving a copperplate. The plate is then mounted in a press which inks the plate, then wipes off the excess leaving ink only in the engraved lines of text. The press then uses enormous pressure to stamp the card and the copperplate together, transferring the ink on to the card, and at the same time raising the image. It is the combination of the tactile appeal of the raised image and the clarity of the fine lines which make engraved invitations the best of all formats.

Potential users of fine engraved work should beware of stationers offering copperplate engraving using computer generated typefaces; they are but a poor relation of the genuine article.

### SUMMARY

Each of the three processes outlined above can be used to produce wedding invitations. The choice of which process to use will be governed by time and funds available and impression desired. By tradition, invitations for weddings are normally on folded card (known as fly card) with the fold running vertically on the left hand and portrait (that is to say tall, rather than wide).

Invitations for receptions, dances, balls, etc. are traditionally on plain card not folded, and are landscape (wide rather than tall).

As a general rule the thicker the card the better, although there are limitations with some processes.

The possible combinations available for those who wish to stray away from the traditional approach are almost unlimited, but the advice of the stationer should always be sought as to what combinations will or will not work. To this end it is certainly advisable to patronise a stationer which has its own factory facilities and can tailor the invitation precisely to your requirements.

# CHAPTER 2

# Photography and Video

A wedding is an important historical occasion in the lives of two families. It is not hard to appreciate why wedding photography has developed as a record of the event for posterity.

Wedding photographs also give family and friends of the couple, as well as the couple themselves, shared memories of the day, to be enlarged and framed.

These two concepts are very different and good photographic coverage of a wedding should fulfil both requirements. A wedding photographer who concerns himself only with providing an accurate record of who was involved in family groupings is not offering the best service.

As well as formal group shots, which should be taken as your historical record, wedding photography should sum up the atmosphere and events of the day as they happen in a natural way. Wedding photographers are so often guilty of trying to create photo opportunities out of situations which are unreal. Why should a bride who has never played the piano in her life be asked to pose, fingers at the ready over the keys, at the piano in all her finery? Nothing could be more irrelevant and unnatural and why would any family want such a photograph?

The best photographic coverage of a wedding is to provide a story of the day from start to finish. As a bride you will not only want proof of what you were there to see with your own eyes. You might like the photographer to seek out and find the groom and his male friends in the morning and keep track of their activities. You might like him to visit you and photograph you and the bridesmaids as you get ready. You should certainly consider photographs of the reception venue and the decorations at the church or synagogue. Wedding days pass all too quickly and many brides comment on the fact that they can hardly remember what the flowers or the food looked like in all the excitement.

You might like to consider any of the following topics:

Bride and attendants getting ready;

Groom and attendants getting ready;
Preparations for the reception;
Flowers and decoration;
Guests arriving in groups for the ceremony;
The ceremony itself;
Formal historical photographs of family groups;
Informal groups;
Formal reception shots – cake, speeches etc.;
Informal reception shots – friends in groups and conversation;
Bride and groom leaving;
General atmosphere.

It is easy to appreciate that to meet all these requirements would be a difficult task for a single photographer working alone and it is true to say that the best wedding coverage is always provided by two or more photographers working together so that they are not required to be in more than one place at any one time. However, there is no reason why an efficient, experienced single photographer could not manage the greater part of this with help and forward planning from you.

CHOOSING THE RIGHT PHOTOGRAPHER

There is an enormous number of photographers who 'specialise' in wedding photography. Any professional in this field should be able to provide a good photograph of any subject. Technical skill and adaptability are things which you might justifiably expect. Far more important, however, is the attitude of the professional as he goes about his work. Understanding how to deal with brides and grooms and their families when so much is going on and often under considerable pressure can only come with experience, so do always use someone experienced in weddings.

You should ask to see examples of the work of any photographer you are thinking of booking. What you actually get for your money can vary considerably. Some photographers provide an album of photographs, ready developed and enlarged, chosen by them from the shots taken during the day.

The trouble is, what someone considers to be a lovely photograph of you is rarely the choice you would make if given the chance. Others charge per photograph taken which can be hard to assess. Rarely do you get to see all the photographs taken during the day which can be a great shame.

Different approaches to photography do affect the picture taken. Some photographers take a very lyrical approach, often misting the edges of the photograph to add a softly romantic feel. Others take a much more journalistic approach, allowing you to choose your own enlargements from the films they will develop in snapshot size first while you decide.

To find the right photographer for you, see as many as you can realistically manage, look at their work, discuss their prices and adaptability and your preferences.

## COST

Wedding photographers will often submit several different prices based on different degrees of coverage. One who is with you all day, perhaps for as much as twelve hours, will naturally want to charge a higher price than one who will be there for four hours and leave half-way through the reception. This is something you need to know. It would be a great shame to plan an amazing departure from your reception and not know at the time that you had booked a photographer whose price only covered his staying for the first couple of hours. Be sure to have a guaranteed agreement on this point before agreeing a fee.

The price you pay a photographer will cover their services on the day and usually a certain number of photographs in any of the forms mentioned. Further copies and enlargements will be charged separately and you need to know exactly what the price will be for these. There would be little point in using a photo-grapher who wanted so much money for reprints that you are embarrassed to offer copies to your friends and families. It is very easy to match, if not surpass, the price you will already have paid for the attendance of the photographer on the day, in reprints and copies and enlargements.

If you know that you would like several sets of the wedding photographs developed at the same time, tell the photographer you are using before the wedding, as each set will be much cheaper, just like holiday photographs. You never know how many brownie points you could score by presenting a full set to your fiancé's family as well as your own.

## COPYRIGHT

Legally, the copyright of any photograph remains the property of the photographer unless arranged otherwise. This means that the negatives of the photographs taken at your wedding belong to the photographer and not to you. It is in the financial interests of any photographer to hold on to the negatives given the significant income they can continue to generate after the wedding. Nobody could argue with the right of any photographer to hold on to negatives for this purpose, provided that the costs of copies is reasonable. The problem is rather that if, in ten years' time, you have lost your favourite wedding photograph or it has become damaged, and you cannot locate the original photographer, you will be stuck and have no chance of replacing it. All brides and grooms should consider an arrangement with their wedding photographer so that they keep the negatives of their own wedding day. If the photographer wants to keep them as a professional record, do remember that negatives can also be copied.

PLANNING

All of us must at some time have been guests at weddings where the behaviour of photographers throughout the event would make us believe that they were the most important person present. They will herd the families into groups with bullish aggression, while messing around with unwieldy tripods, use flashes at crucial moments when binding promises are being made and keep guests waiting interminably while they try to get the right shots. Even worse, they can insist that things are redone because they missed it the first time.

There is just no need for any of this stupid and inappropriate behaviour, but brides and grooms are often equally to blame in this respect. You must tell a photographer exactly what you want done and how, or suffer the consequences. Use your team meetings to agree on a list of photographs of families and friends that you know you will want taken, particularly with reference to what happens after the ceremony. This will mean that the photographer can achieve all he must far quicker. Prime the families, make sure they know not to wander off and chat to friends immediately after the service, but to organise themselves with the help of the best man. DO NOT keep your guests waiting and watching a neverending flurry of confusion and chaos. Plan to have the photographs taken in 15 minutes and no more, plan which you want taken and give this list to the photographer in advance. If you would like some black and white photographs taken too, let him know this. Give him an itinerary of events during the reception so that he does not go to the loo just as your father stands up to make his speech.

## PHOTOGRAPHS OF THE CEREMONY

Religious and civil establishments will not always allow photography, even for a wedding, since copyright laws can be infringed. If you want any photographs taken of the actual marriage ceremony, you must ask the minister or Registrar whether permission can be given. Flashes are particularly unpopular and if your photographer will have to get the shots without the use of flash, he will need to know in advance in order to bring the right equipment. The same applies, and to an even greater degree, to video or film coverage.

## VIDEO

Video coverage of a wedding is something brides are either adamantly for or against. As with photographers, using the right company will give the right results and all the same advice must apply. See the work of several companies and put your questions to each before agreeing to anything. Videos can be even more intrusive than photography and bearing in mind the sophistication of the newest equipment, there is equally little excuse.

There is no doubt that film coverage of a wedding conveys more of the atmosphere than stills could hope to achieve and together they are a good balance. If you have a video of the wedding, you must remember that you are under no obligation to watch it every day, but if you do not have one, you can never judge how evocative it might have been. Amateur videos can be just as much, if not more fun than professional videos.

As with photographs, the copyright of a video remains with the cameraman and you may need to indulge in persuasive techniques to be given the master tape. Order the copies you know you will need before the wedding and the price will probably be better.

# CHAPTER 3
# The Cake

As weddings have always involved feasting, so feasts have always involved cakes. The more important the feast, the larger and generally more lavish the cake. Culinary traditions and the celebration food which comes from them are governed by seasonal availability. Celebration food has always consisted of what has, at any one time, been considered special and the wedding cake is a prime example.

In the United Kingdom we have come to associate the traditional wedding cake as being made from a heavy fruit-based dough. It is normally constructed of several tiers of differing sizes. The cake is covered in marzipan to retain its freshness and give a smooth surface to which a decorative icing is then applied. In actual content, the traditional wedding cake is little different from any other celebration cake.

In the past, the act of cutting the wedding cake was the responsibility of the bride alone, who having made the first incision would allow the bridesmaids to take over the task of distributing it in true handmaiden style. This explains why the wedding cake has, at times, been known as the 'bride's cake' and why one is sometimes still featured at weddings today, usually as an addition to the main wedding cake which the couple will cut together in ceremonial fashion. The bride's cake and the wedding cake share the same root as symbols of fertility. The distribution of the cake among the guests is equally symbolic of the sharing of happiness and it is very ill-mannered as a guest to refuse a piece of wedding cake, however small. Even the tiniest crumb will do.

Sharing is an important feature of all religions and the tradition of keeping or sending pieces of cake for friends and family who could not attend the wedding is an ancient one. This is usually managed today with the help of little boxes which can be bought from any large stationer.

The fruit cake used in the construction of a traditional wedding cake has a very long life, which is undoubtedly one of the reasons for its enduring popularity. Up to a point, fruit cake matures with age and wedding cakes are almost always intended to be bigger than the combined appetites of the guests so that uneaten cake can be kept. The top tier of a wedding cake is almost always kept complete, even today, to be re-iced and eaten on the couple's first anniversary or the occasion of the christening of their first child, which in years gone by would probably have coincided as a consequence of the marriage. If you plan to follow this tradition and intend to store your unused cake, you should consult the baker on the best method.

## ALTERNATIVES TO THE TRADITIONAL

Rich and heavy fruit cake is not everyone's first choice and many brides prefer to opt for a lighter or more interesting alternative. More and more cake specialists are consequently putting together combinations of tiers made from different cake bases, to suit a variety of tastes. Although having exactly the same outward appearance as a traditional wedding cake, the actual content could have a fruit layer, and several sponge layers incorporated within the overall design.

Sometimes it is the very traditional appearance of the wedding cake which puts a bride off. There are alternatives.

*The Croquembouche 'crunch in the mouth'*

This is the traditional French celebration cake eaten at all important family occasions. It is, in essence, a tower or pyramid of choux buns (profiteroles), filled with delicious, flavoured creams and drenched in caramel, peanut brittle and usually spun sugar.

The construction of the Croquembouche requires not only great patience but great skill to stop it becoming lopsided and toppling over. French bakers have a national pride in their baking traditions and it is always better to ask an authentic French baker to construct a Croquembouche. Not only does he or she need dextrous accuracy, but because the cake contains fresh cream, it must be made and served very fresh.

Unlike traditional fruit cakes, Croquembouches do not contain costly ingredients. You pay rather for the skill and time of the baker. Before choosing to have a Croquembouche for your wedding, do think about logistics. If the cake cannot be delivered to you on the morning of the wedding, someone will have to pick it up and transporting such a fragile and all important part of the wedding over any distance can be very hard indeed – a Croquembouche for 100 people will be at least three to four feet high!

Brides and grooms do not exactly cut the Croquembouche, since it would be impossible to break through the rock hard caramel and brittle. The tradition instead is that the bride whacks it with a little hammer to break the surface and allow the buns to be separated. It is very nice for the couple to follow the tradition of actually serving the guests themselves. Do remember that Croquembouches are sticky and difficult to eat with the fingers, unlike fruit cake, and you will need little plates and preferably forks for all the guests.

Naturally you cannot send pieces of Croquembouche to absent friends, so bear this in mind when making your choice.

*Themed cakes*

Almost any shape can be made in cake, depending on the cake base used and the sculptural talents of the baker. If the idea of the traditional shape of a wedding cake is not for you, you could consider something different.

Themed cakes are best chosen when there is an obvious theme to the wedding or when the theme chosen for the cake has some direct bearing on the wedding. There is a tradition, again in France, of wedding cakes made in the shape of the church in which the couple are married. Buildings are ideal for cakes. A vivid personal memory is of a wedding cake made as an exact replica of the Chateau in the Loire where the groom proposed to the bride. At the reception, this incredible cake was put on a tiny stage in the middle of the room and spotlit to dramatic effect.

*Wedding cakes and specialities from other countries*
Any country will offer inspiration for the wedding cake and any bride marrying someone from another country has the perfect excuse to investigate and use what she might find to her advantage.

No Italian feast, for example, would ever be complete without a glorious Cassata – a layered sponge and ice cream bombe set with nuts and fruits. Ice cream wedding cakes are little known here but can be glorious for hot, summer weddings. There are a number of specialist ice cream manufacturers who will make ice cream wedding cakes and they are always delicious since the ice cream is always home-made. Made in ice cream, a wedding cake can faithfully resemble the traditional shape and colour and contain a myriad selection of fruit sorbets and other flavours under the white vanilla outer shell. You cannot keep ice cream wedding cake and you certainly cannot send pieces to friends. It is important to think about the melting factor and to seek advice on this from whoever makes it for you. It is not always possible for an ice cream wedding cake to be on display throughout the reception, but do not discount the dramatic effect of having it brought out in splendour at the appropriate moment.

At the root of many international wedding treats is the almond. Sugared almonds are delicacies all over the world and especially for weddings. They can be bought in every colour imaginable and are very useful for colour themes. Either scattered loosely on to tables or placed into tiny net bags or bowls, these are little gifts or 'favours' from the bride to her guests.

In your choice of wedding cake, spend some time thinking about the options available to you and how sensible or appropriate each might be. Look for inspiration and you will doubtless find it.

## A FAVOURITE RECIPE

(Instead of fruit cake)
# Traditional Ginger Cake
(with fruit & nut)

2 × 7" square tins or 2 × 8" round tins

| | |
|---|---|
| 8oz butter | 2 level tsp bic. of soda |
| 12oz black treacle | 4 level tsp ground ginger |
| 4oz golden syrup | 1 tsp fresh grated ginger |
| ½ pint of milk | 4oz sultanas |
| 4 eggs | 4oz raisins |
| 1lb plain flour | 2oz chopped walnuts |
| 4oz brown sugar | 1 tbsp rum |
| 2 tsp mixed spice | |

Using a large saucepan, warm together butter, treacle and syrup. Add milk and allow mixture to cool. Beat eggs and add to cooled mixture. Sieve flour and place in a bowl together with sugar, mixed spices, bicarbonate of soda, ground ginger and fresh ginger. Add the cooled mixture and blend in with a spoon. Add the fruit and nuts and rum and mix thoroughly. Turn into two greased and lined tins. Bake on the middle shelf at Mark 2, 310° F for 1¼–1½ hours.

### Filling

| | |
|---|---|
| 12oz demerara sugar | 1 tsp vanilla essence |
| ¼ pint milk | pinch of bicarbonate of soda |
| 1oz butter | 2oz chopped walnuts |

Put the milk and sugar into a saucepan over a low heat. When the sugar is dissolved, boil briskly until a temperature of 230° is reached. Remove the pan from the heat, add the butter, essence and bicarbonate of soda. Beat until the mixture thickens. Spread over the cooked cakes and sprinkle with chopped walnuts.

## CHAPTER 4
# Transports of Delight

Unless you are fortunate enough to live literally next door to the church, synagogue or register office in which your marriage will take place, or you are combining a civil ceremony with your reception venue, you will need to think about how and in what you and the other members of the bridal party travel between these two (and often more) geographical points. You may feel the need to arrive in grand state even at a civil marriage.

## 1. Cars

### SERIOUSLY GRAND CARS
For many brides their wedding day represents the perfect opportunity to indulge in hiring a wonderful car that will appropriately reflect the care they will have taken on their appearance and the importance of the occasion. If you take the time to search and you start your search early enough, you would probably find that you were able to book virtually any make, model, age and colour of car that you could possibly dream of. Luxury cars with space enough in the back for the grandest frock are still probably most popular for weddings. Rolls-Royce, Bentley and other limousines are quite easy to

find from local car hire firms. Most hire companies will have at least one white or cream model, sometimes vintage, sometimes modern, which is kept up especially for weddings. White and cream cars can be booked up well in advance, so if you know that the colour is important to you, do not delay.

## Fun Cars
Less formal weddings or those for which the bride and groom are determined to be a little different are the ideal reason to look further than to the classic white limousine. There are a number of firms that specialise in classic American cars and other interesting models from about 1920 onwards, in all sorts of fascinating shapes and colours.

Vintage London taxis from the 1930s come in blues and clarets complete with luggage rack at the back and just about enough space for two occupants – not recommended for big dresses – but charming nonetheless. They would be ideal for leaving the reception once you have changed into something more manageable.

Sleek Cadillacs and convertibles from the 1950s add a touch of flair to any wedding and will often score myriad points with the groom. New York Police Department cars, complete with flashing lights and sirens or yellow and black chequered New York taxis certainly make a statement. You can even find real rock star cars with blacked out windows, built in televisions and bars. Think about what would be right for you and try to find it.

## Pricing
Car hire firms operate in several ways. The most straightforward of these methods is by charging the customer an hourly rate which will include the chauffeur's fees and more or less unlimited mileage. This sort of service is often only available on cars which are not specifically kept for use at weddings, but it can be more cost-effective to only pay for the use you need.

Other companies charge a set fee for a wedding car, which will give you use of the car for up to a certain number of hours and within a limited distance. The older the car, the less the owners will want it driven, so mileage can be very limited if you are not to incur extra costs. Whether you require the car for the full allotment of hours or not, you will be asked to pay the cost, which can be expensive. It is, however, the only guarantee the company has that they will make as much profit from hiring the car in question to you as compared to another bride on the same day, who might need it for a longer period of time.

## DEALING WITH CAR HIRE FIRMS

No one will be able to supply you with a quotation unless you have a pretty good idea of the timings and addresses in question, so do remember to have the information they are likely to need to hand when you start making contact. The price charged will depend on the day of the week, the time of year, the distance to be covered and how long you require the car for, as well as the actual model of car. When you are quoted a price, it is important to know how many hours use it

will give you and to calculate your timings correctly. The time can start from when the driver arrives, which should always be a good twenty minutes or so before you are due to leave, so remember to add this on to your required time. Find out whether the price covers payment for the driver and what sort of uniform he will be wearing. Check on whether the company intends to decorate the car with ribbons on the front and flowers in the back and tell them if you would prefer not to have these. Check what the procedure would be for replacing the car and what alternatives they could offer should your chosen car be involved in an accident or break down.

## PEOPLE TO ACCOUNT FOR

So far we have been discussing transport for you, the bride. It is left up to the groom to make travel arrangements for himself and the best man to get to the church, synagogue or register office. He is also traditionally responsible for organising the car for himself and his new wife from the ceremony to the reception. It is quite normal, however, for the car that has taken the bride to the ceremony to wait and to then take the couple on to the reception. Having in most cases arrived before the bride, the groom will probably not see the car she arrives in, which offers brides all sorts of scope for surprising their husbands as they emerge from the ceremony.

It is not always possible to keep the same car all through the day to take the couple away again from the reception. This may be negotiable, but it will always be more expensive.

As well as the two of you, there are other members of the families whose travel you will need to arrange. No one should really plan to drive themselves. Apart from the obvious problems of parking, drinking and driving and security, driving ruins shoes and creases clothing. Let someone else do the work.

The bride's mother will normally arrive at the ceremony in advance of her daughter and traditionally travels with the bridesmaids and other attendants. The bride would then follow on accompanied by only her father. If the distance between the pick up point and the ceremony is considerable, two cars will be needed. The bride cannot be kept waiting and be made late for the ceremony because the car which should have returned after dropping her mother is stuck in traffic.

Other relatives may need to be transported, depending on

your situation. Grandparents are natural considerations and it is certainly courteous and thoughtful to offer help if the travel poses any significant problems for them.

Ian Douglass from Fleetwood Limousines gives his thoughts on car hire:

FLEETWOOD LIMOUSINES

Traditionally, brides have favoured white Rolls-Royces and Daimlers and very fine cars they are, too. But more and more, brides want something different. Our options range from the 'Best of British Collection' to fine American cars, perhaps from the 1940s and 1950s. For those who insist that only something really old will do, pre-war cars, Bugattis, Hispano-Suizas, British limousines and coach-built American vehicles all add their own style to your wedding.

You may want to arrive like an American President of the past in a long limousine with running boards, whitewall tyres and split windscreen. Or you might prefer a yellow convertible straight from Beverly Hills as your own car for the day. Alternatively, if you want a white Rolls, consider a convertible Silver Cloud, a rare beauty.

But remember, if you want a convertible, getting married in November is not the best time to choose and nearly all convertibles have only two doors. If your perfect wedding dress is full and flowing, access needs to be checked carefully. Stepping elegantly in and out for your photographer and guests can only then be accomplished in a four door saloon or limousine.

Seven tips to remember when hiring your wedding car:

● Book early. Some cars get reserved more than a year in advance.

● Make sure that you are dealing with a reliable and reputable company that will not let you down at the last minute. Old cars do break down but some companies let it happen through negligence and bad maintenance. You can usually tell the standard of cars available by how well they are maintained.

- If you have any doubts about the choice of car, insist on asking for a photograph or arranging an appointment to see it. Then you can be sure you have exactly what you want.

- If you want a second car for family and bridesmaids, talk to your hire company about an all-in deal at a special price. They should be helpful. If you are booking that second car, check how many people it can carry. Six in addition to the driver is usually the maximum figure and you don't want to disappoint passengers or crush people's clothes.

- Send a clear map of your preferred route to the hire company in advance. That way there will be no last minute confusions about turning right instead of left. Always make sure that they have the bride's telephone number.

- If you live in a street where it is difficult to park, try to reserve a space. Neighbours are usually very helpful. That way you know that your car will be right outside when you want it and if, by any mischance, it should rain, you have the shortest possible distance to walk.

- Should you want any special facilities in the car, for example champagne for yourself and the groom on the way to the reception, inform your hire company well in advance. They will usually be very happy to oblige.

Follow these tips and you will have no worries. And remember too, that unlike some churches, most hire companies have no objection to the throwing of rice or confetti. That great picture of you and your new husband getting into your ideal car in a shower of confetti, surrounded by family and friends, can be yours for ever.

## 2. Other forms of transport

So far we have only discussed cars as a method of bridal transport. Carriages can be very simple or very grand and are therefore suitable for all types of weddings. Choosing an open carriage can be risky weather-wise and even if there is a hood, the process of having to put it up can ruin the idyllic look and make it quite hard to see out, let alone to be seen as you progress in your regal splendour. If you decide on a carriage, try to go and see the choices before you commit yourself or find that you have left it too late for an alternative.

## HOT AIR BALLONS
Few brides would be either mad enough or brave enough to plan to arrive in a hot air balloon, but plenty of couples are tempted by the idea of leaving their reception in one. It is of course a spectacular departure and an expensive one and there will be restrictions as to when and where it is feasible. Hot air balloon companies can usually be found in local telephone directories.

## HELICOPTERS AND PRIVATE AIRCRAFT
Being whisked away in a helicopter or private plane is as glamorous if not as sedate an exit as a hot air balloon. Even greater restrictions are likely to apply, so plenty of thought and time need to go into investigating either option.

## BOATS
If your wedding reception is to take place near water of any kind, you might like to think about using a boat as transport at some point. Even a large stream running through the garden is often enough water to allow an energetic groom to row his new wife out of sight in a tiny flower-bedecked rowing boat. Once out of view, there is nothing to stop the couple from leaping out and into a car for the rest of the journey, but your guests would forever remember your romantic departure. If the stream is slow flowing and night has fallen, candles can be floated in the water around the boat, to drift along with the current.

## WALKING
A bride who can consider walking to her wedding or back again, husband in tow, leading a procession of smiling guests is extremely lucky. To not have to get into cars again, but to allow the ceremony to flow naturally on to the reception in this manner is the nicest possible thing imaginable.

You do, however, need contingency plans for rain, so do think about how and in what you would get to the ceremony and back again just in case.

### TRANSPORT FOR GUESTS

Unless your wedding or reception is in a truly inaccessible place, to which normal public transport services do not run, unless parking is impossible and taxis are not available or any great distance needs to be travelled between the two locations, you are under no obligation to provide transport for your guests.

Some families do decide to arrange transport for guests for these or other reasons, but in general the decision is made because if it was not, nobody would be likely to be able to come, which would rather defeat the object!

If for any reason you do decide to provide transport for your guests to the reception, think about ways you could get the atmosphere going while they are en route. Having drinks served on a bus or coach or even a boat will lessen the pain of travel. Mini coaches are ideal for smaller numbers. Do not discount a fleet of taxis in convoy.

# CHAPTER 5
# Wedding Presents

Gifts presented to a bride and groom by those attending the wedding and marking the importance of the occasion are an ancient and universal tradition.

In different times and different cultures, wedding guests have sometimes contributed to the costs of the feasting either financially or by the provision of food of some sort. At other times the couple have been showered with money and symbolic gifts. Even today in some cultures, money is given or pinned on to the clothing of the couple as they eat or dance.

In our tradition, wedding presents are functional, forming part of a general collection of items to furnish the home in which the couple will live.

A gift may be sent as soon as an engagement is announced but will not usually be sent until a date has been set for the wedding and invitations distributed.

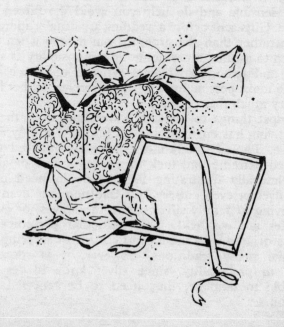

## 1. The wedding present list

Wedding presents are not a tax payable by the guest in return for an invitation to the wedding. They are given as a mark of affection and often chosen with great care. It is very important that couples are seen to respect the basis on which gifts are sent and that they do not think of making a choice of gifts they would like to receive as their ultimate right. It is ill-mannered, tactless and incorrect to include any reference to presents you would like to receive or where these may be found when you send your invitations. It would be rather like sending a friend an invitation to a birthday party and including a list of presents you would like them to choose from. It would seem greedy and you would not think of such a thing. If the friend was to ask what you might like, it would be perfectly alright to specify, but not until such a question is raised. So it should be with weddings. There is a burgeoning trend for reference to the wedding list to be included in the invitation, which is a deplorable practice encouraged by shops offering a wedding list service and by a bride's natural wish for expediency.

There is nothing mean, greedy or nasty about making a list. The lapse in etiquette is to ram it down everybody's throat. Lists are sensible and do help you avoid the fifteen toaster syndrome. Gifts sent before a wedding are usually addressed to the bride rather than the groom, from a time when women were given to assume more domestic responsibility as a matter of course and without complaints. Whether or not a bride ever intends to make personal use of the saucepans on her list, this is still very much the tradition.

Like most things to do with a wedding, even the act of present giving has customs and traditions that may come as a surprise. Though thankfully not widely adhered to, it is considered extreme bad luck to ask for knives or anything sharp. Naturally frustrating for anyone in need of good chef's knives or even cutlery, this tradition may even extend to the giving of family silver where the knives, or even just the blades are withheld. This particular prejudice seems mistily associated with the idea of cutting or severing friendship. Like many traditions, however, it is more likely founded in practicality, since silver knife blades are so susceptible to damage, they need to be renewed once a generation.

## PUTTING TOGETHER A LIST

Drawing up a coherent list of the items you can realistically specify as wedding presents is a far harder task than you might imagine. If you are setting up home for the first time, on the one hand you need absolutely everything and on the other you are unlikely to get absolutely everything, so your choices need consideration. If you already have a well-equipped home, you will find that many of the more obvious gaps typically suitable for wedding presents have already been filled. In either case you must be sure to specify a wide range of gifts to suit all budgets.

## WHAT SORT OF LIST?

The first sort of wedding list you might consider is pretty basic and gives a broad outline of the items involved. It might specify certain colours or types but in general will leave the final choice of items up to the guests themselves. It might read:

Dinner service – six place settings, blue and white
Cutlery – silver plate for six place settings
Bathtowels × 2 – plain white cotton
etc.

Once the couple have put the list together, it is usually given to the bride's mother, so that when a guest telephones to find out about the list, as any experienced wedding guest will do, they can be guided through the choices and have their decision crossed off the list.

This sort of do-it-yourself list does include an element of risk because you cannot assume that any guest will necessarily be able to judge your taste and what you receive might not be at all what you had in mind. Be as specific as possible in the items you choose and if necessary, give the maker's name or stock name or number. You will never avoid the odd rogue gift, but if someone chooses to give you something they have thought of themselves, it would be rude to accept it with anything other than gratitude and respect.

## SHOP LISTS

The other sort of wedding list which is more common and extremely popular is one held at a particular shop or department store. Almost all larger shops offer a wedding list service nowadays, designed to help you and boost their sales at the same time. You register with the appropriate department and are generally given a catalogue or form with which to wander at leisure through the shop. When you see what you want, you either fill in the appropriate bit of the form or make a note of the stock number and how many of each item you want, depending on the method used. Having completed the task, which can take ages, you file your choices with the bridal registration department and wait.

When your guests telephone your family, they are given the name and telephone number of the shop or shops in question. They then have the choice of visiting the shop and seeing the items you have chosen before making their own choice, or they can simply telephone. They will be guided over the telephone by an assistant who will explain the different choices in each department, i.e. china, cutlery, and the various price ranges available. Having come to a decision, they can visit the shop and pay for the present. There is little or no risk of duplication of presents if the list is held at a shop since the items are struck off as they are chosen.

## Realism
Make an initial list before you set off for the shop. If you do not, you risk being waylaid and tempted by all sorts of unnecessary things which you might well regret when they, rather than what you do really want and need, start arriving through the door. This list, agreed between you both, before you start will help to avoid the typical rows, as exhaustion takes its toll.

## Delivery of presents
Delivery of presents bought from a wedding list is usually free so long as it can be arranged to take place during normal working hours. Some shops deliver everything the moment it is bought. Others notify the bride that the present has been chosen but wait until a sufficient quantity has been chosen to make a delivery worthwhile. Remember that whatever address is given for the delivery of presents, someone will need to be at home when they arrive. Never allow presents to be left on doorsteps or in back gardens. You may need to ask a parent, friend or neighbour to allow you to use their address rather than your own for just this reason. When presents do arrive

they should be unpacked immediately to check for any damage. Damaged goods will be replaced by the shops in question, but your chances of this diminish as time goes on.

## When to make the list

If you are observing the standard 8–12 week warning period for invitations, the list should be drawn up or placed at a shop by the time the invitations go out. Some guests are very quick about responding to invitations and getting their gift for the couple sorted out and it would be foolish to miss the opportunity. If for any reason you decide to send your invitations out much earlier, you could find that shops are not keen to allow you to register so far in advance of the wedding. This will be because of stock changes and it is disappointing to specify something on a wedding list and find that two or three months later, it is no longer carried as stock so no one can buy it for you.

## Sending letters of thanks

However humble or majestic, every present you receive must be marked by a personal, handwritten letter of thanks, as soon as possible after it is received or you have been notified that it has been chosen for you and this means before the wedding as well as afterwards. Sending a ready printed card is not an acceptable alternative. Start your thank you letters as soon as presents begin to arrive and you will find the task far less daunting.

## Displaying your presents

If your wedding is to take place at home, you might like to follow an old tradition of displaying the presents in one room for the guests to inspect the booty. It is increasingly difficult for today's bride to follow this because the great majority of wedding gifts may not arrive until after the wedding and the table could look a little bare. Guests who actually take or bring their presents to the reception are not always wise to do so. The couple will not have time to open them during the reception and in some cases, for weeks afterwards and it only means that someone has to take charge of them and make sure that they get to their final destination. There are always some guests who will bring their gifts and your chief bridesmaid should be primed and ready with a roll of sellotape to ensure that cards marking the donor do not get separated from the present, thereby making it impossible for you to know who to thank. Wedding presents must be put somewhere secure as it is easy for someone to walk off with them. However miserable, it can happen.

Friends who are unable to come to your wedding may still send a gift in which case you must remember to send an extra special letter of thanks in return, remarking upon their kindness.

## Can you ask for money?

In a word, no. Even if you and your groom have been living together for years and have everything you need. Only your families might consider contributing to something other than domestic requirements. Guests can never be asked to pay into a general fund. If there is nothing you need, ask for nothing.

## Exchanging presents

Duplicate or unloved wedding presents may be exchanged, but never without notifying the original donor first and giving some suitable euphemistic excuse. If you exchange wedding presents on the quiet, when the friend or relative comes to your house expecting to see their cut glass punchbowl proudly displayed on your sideboard, and doesn't, you are in big trouble.

## Bridal showers

These are an American custom and are really nothing more than simple gatherings of friends of the bride, usually female, involving the giving of small personal rather than domestic gifts. Ideal presents are indulgent bath products or simple little things chosen with the individual bride in mind.

## Professional wedding list services

There are a number of companies who will take charge of your wedding list. The way in which they work differs from one to the other, but in general they offer an excellent service. By buying direct from the manufacturer, they will offer items to the couple's guests at the normal retail price, making their profit on the difference, so there is usually no charge for the service, but all brides must check this at the time. The variety of styles and lines of goods may not be as varied as those which are found in the larger department stores, but if anything, this could be a help rather than a hindrance. If a company of this type does exist in your area, you would be wise to check them out. The service offered is usually extremely attentive and more personal than that which is offered by shops, which will deal with far too many lists every year to compete in this respect.

# CHAPTER 6

# The Honeymoon

The wedding journey, or honeymoon, as we now call it, has always been a chance for the newly married couple to enjoy privacy (and in times past the opportunity to get to know each other), and relaxation after the busy period leading up to their wedding.

A hundred years ago, the honeymoon would have had a far greater significance for the bride than it does perhaps today and would have traditionally lasted one month. It is so called because the feelings of the couple for one another during the wedding journey were supposed to equate to the phases of the moon. It must also be remembered that it was the ultimate duty of a wife to also become a mother as soon as possible and to produce a son and heir. One month would have given fair chance of a successful result.

No young bride of the past would have been likely to be an experienced traveller and certainly any travel she had undertaken would not have been without a suitable chaperone. The wedding journey would have given her what must often have been the first glimpse of the world outside the heavily protected environment in which she would have been brought up.

As a married woman, she would now have her place in society and would finally be able to make a few decisions for herself. The honeymoon would also be her first time alone with her husband. Even during engagements, couples were seldom left alone together in a room for fear of something untoward or inappropriate taking place.

Responsibility for the honeymoon has always fallen on the groom for the simple reason that his wife, from her inevitable lack of education, would probably have little or no idea of where they might go. In any case, husbands made the decisions and it was a wife's duty to accept unquestioningly.

Modern honeymoons still give contemporary couples the chance to rest and recuperate after all the hard work they will have put into their weddings and few couples would consider doing without this winding down period, however well they already know each other. It is a tradition that the bride is not told where she is going on her honeymoon, but it is not one that is necessarily adhered to and many brides would really rather know so that they can plan ahead.

Any groom who does plan to keep the destination a secret will have to think about telling the chief bridesmaid or a close friend of the bride. No one, least of all a bride on her honeymoon, wants to find herself at one of those incredibly smart resorts where everyone dresses up for dinner with only the shorts and old T-shirts she has been told she will need for a beach holiday.

## FINANCIAL REALISM

From the moment the couple make the decision to marry, the cost clock starts to tick. Honeymoons, like weddings, have to be planned with regard to the future financial responsibilities of marriage. Even assuming the bride's family has paid the costs of the wedding, both she and her groom must give thought to the lifestyle they will adopt after the wedding. The fact that a honeymoon is a unique experience in the relationship is often guilty of encouraging unwise extravagance without due consideration for the future.

## TIME AND DISTANCE

Professional responsibilities may well mean that a bride and groom cannot take as much time for their honeymoon as they would ideally wish.

The effort of planning a wedding and the emotional

excitement mean that they are exhausted and thought must be given to restful activities. Trying to go too far away in a short time or trying to do too much while you are away will only add to your tiredness. Jet lag can be very debilitating for anyone not used to long-distance travel. Try to give yourself a couple of days clear on the return trip to acclimatise to normal life before returning to work.

PASSPORTS AND VISAS

These should always be checked for validity well in advance and with enough time to spare to solve any problems. Visas are not required for travel to all parts of the world but many favourite holiday destinations do require them. Travelling on a British or European Community passport allows greater freedom of visa-free travel than many other passports, so if you are marrying someone of a different nationality, they may well need visas which you do not.

Grooms will normally book honeymoon tickets in the name of Mr and Mrs. . . Brides will not always have had the time or energy to have their passports amended to their married names before the wedding in which case they will need to remember to travel with their marriage certificate to prove their identities if necessary.

INJECTIONS, INOCULATIONS AND DISEASES

Travel to many destinations involves recommended inoculations against certain diseases. Travel agents, airlines and relevant foreign embassies will be able to advise on the current suggested inoculations, as will most doctors. Some of these require two or more doses over a period of time, so this consideration should not be left to the last minute. Disease epidemics can also travel fast and change the nature of their resistance to the various drugs which are constantly being developed to keep them at bay. Consequentially, recommended doses may be changed at a moment's notice and even if you have recently travelled to your intended destination and have previously had all the injections etc., you may need to check that you are still protected.

INSURANCE COVER AND MEDICAL EMERGENCIES

Any form of foreign travel, however close to home, should never be undertaken without proper travel and medical insurance cover. Most travel agents will insist upon this as a matter of course and their prices could well include a consideration for this. In the United Kingdom we are extremely fortunate and secure in the knowledge that no matter where we are, we will qualify for immediate and free emergency medical treatment. This is not the case in many other countries and even in countries in the European Union, in which British citizens qualify for medical treatment the same as any national, it is rarely free.

Insurance policies will normally involve the insured paying the initial medical costs to be reimbursed upon their return and upon proof being given of the costs involved in the form of receipts or invoices. This means that you should always have an emergency fund over and above what you plan and expect to spend. Credit cards are widely accepted all over the world but not all are accepted in all countries. Do find out which you will be able to use.

OTHER EMERGENCIES

However carefully you plan a honeymoon and however sensibly you behave while you are there, it is possible to find yourself in difficult or emergency situations. Language problems can make matters even worse. British citizens abroad can call upon the consular section of the British Embassy or High Commission in the local capital, or upon the British Consulate or Deputy High Commission to be found in some provincial centres. If you are going very far away it could be wise to find out where these are situated in relation to your destination.

WHO TO TRAVEL WITH?

Most honeymoons will be booked through travel agents specialising in a certain type of holiday or travel to certain parts of the world. The level of service and experience offered by different travel agents can vary enormously so it is always better to travel with an agent who has an established reputation. Not all travel agents are members of supervisory associations such as A.B.T.A. (the Association of British Travel Agents) and any disappointment you feel will be harder to express and even harder to rectify after the fact.

One travel agent with many years of experience in helping

couples plan their honeymoons is Abercrombie and Kent. Here are some questions they have put together for you to ask yourself and come to the best conclusion:

---

HONEYMOONS WITH ABERCROMBIE & KENT

Our aim is to allow you to indulge in your wildest fantasies but to convert them into a reasonably logical trip. To help us plan your dream honeymoon, here are some questions.

1. Are you thinking of Europe or Worldwide?
2. How long can you be away? 1 week
                              2 weeks
                              More
3. Do you want a) A relaxing beach holiday
              b) Activity/sports
              c) Cultural
              d) Wildlife
              e) Self Drive
              f) Mixture
4. Are you happy to forgo the food and wine versus romantic surroundings?
5. Do you have a budget; are you restricted by how much you spend?
6. Do you mind joining other people as part of a small group for all or part of the time, or wish to be completely on your own?
7. Would you like a true Robinson-Crusoe-type island away from it all or do you like cities?
8. Do you want to stay put in one place or move around?
9. 'A room with a view' can be a special feature.
10. Will you wish to travel on Sunday? This has an important bearing on flights to some of the more remote destinations.
11. Will your wife be travelling on her maiden name or already have her new passport? We require this for air-ticketing.
12. Is it top secret to keep information away from your fiancé(e)?
13. Are you satisfied with a self-catering villa?

14. Will you book your own first night hotel in UK or would you like suggestions from us?
15. How about leaving your reception – by horse and carriage or hot-air balloon?
16. Would you like to upgrade to club or first class on the flight?

# Dress Sense

# CHAPTER 1
# And the Bride Wore . . .

## 1. The wedding dress

Deciding what to wear on your wedding day is probably one of the most difficult decisions you will have to make. If you are not happy, if you are uncomfortable or if you feel in any way conspicuous for the wrong reasons, it will haunt you through the day and beyond. A bride who is confident in the way she looks is a happy bride and a happy bride is an important ingredient of a wonderful wedding.

An inappropriate or ill-suiting wedding dress will be on proud display whenever you catch sight of any of your wedding photographs. There are only too many married women who wince every time they glance round a room and see what should be the proudest and most beautiful photographic trophy. Even brides with a radiant smile and a secure knowledge that they have never looked better may find themselves having a quick attack of embarrassment at their choice of wedding day style after a few years. Fashions change and so does our interpretation. Anyone who delves into the wedding albums of a bride married in the 1960s will probably find her appearance screamingly funny. Eye make-up inspired by Charlie Chaplin, a sheath dress that looks less like a dress and more like a sheath and a hairstyle so teased and burnished as to resemble a fireman's helmet, were just too fashionable to have enduring appeal.

As with everything else, you need to get the basics right. When it comes to the dress, the basic or bottom line is always shape. If the shape does not suit, if you have tried to turn a bamboo pole into an hourglass or a six foot column into a pretty little ball of fluff, you are lost. Knowing the shape that suits is usually instinctive. No amount of lace frills, sparkling beads or tulle can disguise a dress that is architecturally wrong. On the contrary, these will only serve to draw attention to the travesty.

Contemporary fashion dictates the female shape considered ideal at any point in time. Today's bride is in an enviable position in that it is now usual to choose a wedding dress that is inspired in some way by virtually any period in history other than our own. This is a new phenomenon and one that we owe entirely to the most publicised wedding of the century.

Until the blushing Lady Diana Spencer stood at the high altar of St Paul's Cathedral, brides were bound to the whims of contemporary fashion. The world burst into tears of nostalgic joy as she stepped out of the carriage, as fresh and dainty as any fairy tale princess.

David and Elizabeth Emmanuel had not only captured the essence of the bride, but also understood exactly what was appropriate for the occasion. They were the first to turn their backs on *Vogue* and look to the archives for inspiration and in so doing, took the wedding dress firmly back to the future.

There have of course been notable periods in the twentieth century when the fashion and bridal wardrobes have coincided successfully. However, on the whole, as everyday fashions become less and less formal, the bridal gown becomes further removed from real life and more and more isolated as a piece of ceremonial costume. It is all really about dressing up and you will probably have more fun trying wedding dresses out for size and effect than you will have had since childhood dressing-up cupboards.

Larger girls with heavy chests or English pears are at last freed from the tyranny of high hemlines and lycra cling. They can revel in the pinched-in waists, full skirts and generously low necklines that show them for the beautiful, curvy girls they are. Those who bemoan their lanky proportions and lack of bosom can become the Empress Josephine for the day. Suddenly, all those adjectives people have always used to describe you, 'Junoesque', 'Renoiresque', 'willowy' or 'vampy', make sense, as you are put into the right context. Knowing you look good, knowing you will never look better, is 75% of the way to becoming a beautiful bride.

Before you start poring over bridal magazines, visiting dress shops and dressmakers, think about doing a little historical research. Most contemporary wedding dresses borrow heavily from one particular era or another from the last 200 years. Since the changing pace of fashion has accommodatingly provided a different body line for nearly each decade, there will be something for everyone. Use the sources of information available to you to your best advantage. A trip to an art gallery or museum can offer clues not only to shape and body line but also to colour, detail and trimmings. This is not meant as an encouragement to brides to adopt theatrical costume, but merely to establish a basic shape that suits derived from an historical precedent and to treat it with a degree of accuracy. A 1920s inspired dress worn with stiletto heels and a tulle veil is all wrong. If you are going to look historical, then do try to be correct about it or you will end up looking as though you have just walked out of a badly stocked costume shop.

Civil weddings do offer brides a greater degree of freedom in their choice of dress and might well mean that it is possible to get away with a pair of white cycling shorts, but religious ceremonies are traditional and decorous by their very nature and such a disrespectful attitude is not likely to be greeted with total indulgence. If you have nice legs, in fact, if you have particular pride in any part of your body, remember that a glimpse is often more tantalising than an expanse and may introduce just the right note that a short mini could well overplay.

The style adopted by a bride on her wedding day has, throughout history, given an indication of her social and financial status. The more lavish the dress, the more lavish the celebrations in general, particularly the wedding feast. At no stage would a wedding dress of this type not be matched with an equally decorative and costly wedding reception. This is an important point to bear in mind when considering the cost of a wedding dress today. How much is spent on a wedding dress must be in proportion to the overall budget set for the wedding. The basic needs of guests and other demands made on the budget cannot be ignored in favour of a very expensive wedding dress. An ornate and costly wedding dress is out of place at a reception managed on limited means and reveals nothing about the bride other than that she has got her priorities mixed up. Think about what you really should be spending on your dress rather than what you would like to spend.

Only a very small number of brides who think they will have their wedding dress altered or dyed after the wedding to get more than one day's use out of it have actually done so.

The length of a train on a wedding dress has also been

determined by the social standing of the bride marrying and
who she is marrying. Very long trains should only be chosen
for very grand weddings and only if the ceremony is to take
place in a building of similar grandeur. 'Cathedral'-length
trains were only ever intended for long, wide aisles and not for
brides marrying in little country churches. Logic and common
sense are as important in the choice of dress as they are for any
other area of the wedding.

## 2. To buy, to hire or to have it made

Wedding fashions represent an enormous and lucrative international industry. Designers and manufacturers of wedding
dresses borrow heavily from the traditional importance of the
wedding dress in assessing the retail price and often excuse its
cost because of this. Unless a wedding dress is truly well made
and from exceptional fabric, there can be no reason why it
should be greatly more expensive than any other party dress.
As you start to think about where your wedding dress might
come from, be careful not to lose your integrity in your
excitement and let all your normal attention to value for
money slip.

Wedding dresses can be bought 'off the peg', hired or
personally designed and made to measure. These categories
are not all that straightforward and require a little explanation.

Most specific wedding dress designers produce a seasonal
range of styles from which brides can make a choice. What this
essentially means is that each stockist of a particular designer
will hold and display a certain range of dresses in sample sizes
and styles for brides to try on. Having made a choice, the bride
only very rarely actually gets the dress she has tried on.
Normally, her measurements will be taken and an appropriate
size chosen that best matches these measurements, to which
the dress she finally receives is made. For anyone of a fairly
standard size, this approach to which at least one or two
fittings will be added, is usually sufficient to ensure a good fit.
If the bride is not of a standard size, she may well be required
to pay an extra sum to have a pattern cut specially for her to
make sure the dress will be the best possible fit and this service
is often called 'made to measure', which it indeed is.

Brides will find most wedding dress designers very
approachable and that they are able to make personal appointments to discuss their ideas and requirements. This would be

sensible for any bride who likes the designs of a certain designer, but who cannot find the exact dress she wants represented in the selection on display except in component parts. By sitting down with the designer and discussing all the various considerations important to her, the bride will often decide the details herself and have a fairly unique dress as a result and for not much extra cost.

Wedding dresses can also be commissioned from couturiers, or designers whose fashion interests are more broad-based and not restricted only to weddings. International couture houses have an established interest in wedding dresses and few fashion shows do not include some wonderful, if unlikely, interpretation of the wedding dress. If you pick a particular designer, it will probably be because of their established reputation for an individual and sometimes eclectic approach to dressing their clients and this is something you must be prepared to pay significantly more for. No serious or successful couturier could be expected to give the time and attention necessary to one client and one wedding simply out of the goodness of their heart.

At the other end of the scale are the many wedding dresses made every year by a national battalion of private dressmakers and to all budgets. Some will be made to commercially available patterns, others designed specifically for the brides in question and demanding the pattern-cutting skills of the dressmaker. The advantage of using a private dressmaker is clearly based on a compromise of individual style, attention and affordability. The disadvantage with this, or any other form of commission is that until the dress is actually made, it is impossible to know exactly what it will look like on you and this is something you must be aware of, understand and be prepared to accept. Most professional private dressmakers will make a 'toile' first, meaning an exact replica of the dress-to-be, made initially in a cheap fabric, the aim of which is to iron out any problems in the fit or fold of the dress as it will actually be on you. However well cut, a dress made in calico or something similarly cheap will have little bearing on the final impression made by the end product, using silk, satin or velvet and you will have to use your imagination.

Because of the typical very high cost of wedding dresses, an increasing number of brides now consider hiring, rather than buying a dress. Accepting that if they were to buy a dress they would have to tailor their desires to fit a limited budget, and understanding that the dress will only be worn once, they are making a sensible decision, but it is a personal matter. Wedding dress stockists often offer a hire service of some sort although this will not always be suggested by the staff for fear of putting people off buying a dress, which naturally involves a greater profit! Usually, the sample styles and sizes on display can be hired for something like half the retail price of the dress and every effort will be made to ensure that the dress is a good fit and in the best possible condition for the wedding, including having been cleaned and repaired. What it will not be is a brand new dress made to your measurements and to expect anything else would be unreasonable on your part.

Other shops specialise solely in hiring wedding dresses and will generally stock a range that is wide both in terms of style and prices. Naturally, the more expensive the chosen dress was to buy, the greater the price for which it will be hired, but in general hire prices will be more affordable than those offered by stockists whose primary interests lie in actually selling the garment.

### 3. Fabrics

The most popular fabrics for wedding dresses are those which are in some way special and luxurious and therefore often expensive. Silks for summer and satins and velvets for winter are most typical.

However, just because something is made of silk does not mean it has the right to be priced beyond affordability. Raw or Thai silks which are most used in wedding dress manufacture are not in essence all that expensive per metre and especially not if bought in quantity. Be very careful that you do not justify the high cost of a wedding dress on the basis of the fact that it is made of silk. So are plenty of other party dresses without the price tag needing to be read sitting down.

It is also important to remember that all sorts of fabrics can be used to great effect other than simply those mentioned previously. There is nothing wrong with deliciously crisp cottons for summer weddings or woollen crêpe for winter.

While your attention is on the fabric of your wedding

dress, some reference to its colour needs to be made. True, bright white does not suit everybody. Certainly oyster greys, pinks and off whites in particular shades are, at times, more flattering to British skin tones, but this is not necessarily the case and before you discount white entirely, do think about it.

## 4. Veils

Veils have always been associated with the modesty of the bride, and contemporary brides who decide to wear a veil at their weddings will generally do so because of the soft, slightly mystical and magical element it will lend to their appearance.

Not all styles of wedding dress lend themselves easily to the wearing of a veil and some historically-based styles would be positively put out of context by this addition. Any bride would be wise to consider this fact and bear it in mind in choosing her wedding dress.

Veils can be made in a variety of fabrics including silk or nylon tulle, which have very different effects, fine lace, organza

or any other reasonably transparent material. Bridal veils were always intended to cover the face of the bride as she entered a religious building for her marriage, so she does have to be able to see through it enough to be able to walk. Whether a bride chooses to wear a veil over her face rather than just as a frame for it is more a matter of personal choice nowadays although it has to be remembered that certain religious ceremonies expect not only a veil, but for it to cover the face.

Veils may be worn long or short. Traditionally, short veils can drop to the shoulder, waist or finger tip and should be worn if the wedding dress has no train. Following the same principle, long veils should only be worn with dresses which have a train in which case they are supposed to be a foot and a half longer than the dress train. It has never been considered appropriate for a divorcée or widow to wear a veil at her second wedding.

## 5. Accessories

### GLOVES

For many years, even in this century, it was normal for both men and women to wear gloves as part of their daily costume. Because of this, it was not only customary but often considered obligatory for a bride to wear gloves on her wedding day. In order for the wedding ring to be placed on the bride's finger, the fourth finger of the left hand glove would normally be ripped to receive the ring. Gloves are still sometimes chosen by brides today, especially if they will lend authenticity to a particular style of dress, but anyone intending to wear gloves will need to come to a decision as to whether to remove or rip the glove of the hand that is to receive the ring.

### UNDERWEAR

Whether dainty silk or bullet-proof corsetry, what you wear under your wedding dress will be important to the way you look and the way you feel. Certainly, there is always the suggestive symbolism attached to bridal underwear and the wonder of exactly what, if anything, the groom might find as he peels away the layers of finery.

Perhaps more importantly, underwear of the supportive kind may have a part to play in the way in which a dress will fit and the way in which you will carry yourself in it. Straight backs and squarely set shoulders should be part of our posture anyway, but in reality rarely are. They are a must for any bride and will often depend upon a certain amount of assistance. However slender a bride might be, she may well find the added support of a corset or basque under her wedding dress will help her achieve the kind of posture she will be proud to have photographed. We are not used to wearing clothes encompassing a great deal of fabric and wedding dresses can be heavy and cumbersome to wear after a few hours. Extra support across the waist and over the back in the form of boning either in the dress itself or in a corset worn underneath can actually help to make the dress more, rather than less, comfortable.

If you are considering wearing some sort of supportive corsetry, it is important to make the decision before you proceed with the dress. Corsetry can radically alter your shape and will affect the fit of the dress, so it is best to already have the corset before you start trying things on and having fittings. You will need to be certain that the dress does not reveal straps or cleavage levels of the undergarment.

Basques and corsets can be bought inexpensively ready made, or made to measure which is much more expensive but will be important for anyone with a particularly large bust or unusual shape. They must be comfortable and can take some getting used to. Investing in a really well-fitting corset or basque is in many ways more useful than spending too much money on the dress that is to be worn on top of it. Any ballgown or party dress is almost always more flattering if worn on top of a basque and you are quite likely to get many years use out of it any time when shape and posture are especially important to you.

The invention of the most famous contemporary yarn, Lycra, has given modern brides a further option in wedding underpinning. Lycra 'bodies' have been developed in the United States which offer something of the support of old-fashioned corsets and basques without the thickness and with greater comfort and freedom of movement and provide a good compromise.

These are slowly becoming more available in the United Kingdom and will probably have an important part to play for brides in the future.

Petticoats are important to the effect of the overlying fabric of the dress. Many brides decide that they would like a full skirt, but one that is manageable and try, often mistakenly, to reduce the number of layers of petticoat underneath. It is not always a good idea to compromise here as the dress can easily lose the effect for which it was designed. If you do choose a dress or outfit with a full skirt, enjoy its enormity and the rustle it makes as you walk rather than finding reasons to apologise for it.

SHOEMANSHIP

Wedding slippers are as much part of the bridal fairy tale as the dress itself. If your hemline is shorter than ground length, your shoes will naturally show more than they would if you were wearing a full length dress. All wedding shoes should be worn in at home in advance when you do not risk damaging them. However comfortable they may seem to begin with, after the inevitable standing and walking during the wedding day, they can begin to rub and become most uncomfortable.

Silk and satin slippers are the most popular choice for weddings and can be dyed to the exact shade of the wedding dress and this is a service offered by most shoemakers and outlets. They can also be dyed for very different effect and to make a startling statement like Judy Garland in *The Wizard of Oz*, in any jewel colour.

Footwear presents a ready-made opportunity to have fun.

Little bridal toes peeking out from beneath a large skirt are enchanting and a sudden flash of ankle makes you realise just why the Victorians covered the legs of their pianos. A detail on the shoes, a buckle or bow or some embroidery, because it will spend most of its short life below skirt, will catch the light and heighten the excitement when it does emerge. For girls of a more racy nature, who might find all the allusions to blushing brides and trussed up chattels a little tiresome, but who are not into major shock tactics, the style and colour of wedding shoes can be an ideal opportunity for harmless fun.

HOSIERY

Even under a long dress, tights or stockings of some sort should be considered for protection of the feet from rubbing, if nothing else. In fact, bare legs have to be very trim and lovely not to look out of place, even at a summer wedding.

A wide range of hosiery is now available to a bride, some specifically designed for weddings, with ravishing little details included at the ankle, or in delicate laces or silks. There is a danger in going too white in that legs can end up looking bandaged. Flesh-coloured hosiery is often more flattering and less intrusive. Brides should always plan to have more than one pair of tights or stockings for each outfit they are planning to wear for the wedding just in case excitement makes them put their beautifully manicured nails through the delicate yarn.

HANDBAGS

It can be quite a difficult task to imagine where and in what way a bag of some description might fit into the clothing of a bride, either stylistically or practically. To overcome this problem, some brides have what is known rather inappropriately as a 'Dolly bag', or little soft round bag made in the dress fabric and with a drawstring that will fit around her wrist and contain the bare essentials of what she is likely to need to have with her during the day.

In reality, other than perhaps having a special little pocket sewn into the underside of a skirt, there is no sensible alternative except in asking a friend, bridesmaid or relative to keep whatever you think you will need in their bag or pocket, which will usually be the simplest answer.

## HATS

These are still popular alternatives to veils and there are times when the expanse of a large wedding dress needs the balance of something to avoid the 'pinhead effect'. Contemporary wedding dress designers often produce a range of hats to match specific outfits, with a choice of styles to suit different brides. If an outfit is designed to go with a particular hat it would always be sensible to consider wearing the two together before opting for a veil instead. For example, there is an enduring fashion for bridal outfits that echo the riding habits of yesteryear, which can be immensely flattering, but if these are to be put into context and worn correctly, the top hats designed to match them are important.

## BUTTONS AND BOWS

If you have ever wondered why so many wedding dresses are designed with a veritable regiment of little covered buttons up the back, in drill formation, or laced and ribboned and eyeletted, you will probably have answered that they are intended to break the nails of the chief bridesmaid as she struggles to get you in and cause tears of impatient frustration from the groom as he struggles to get you out again.

So many wedding dresses are based on designs from the golden age of romantic dressing, when zips and other less labour-intensive fastenings were either not known or not available to the average dressmaker. A wedding dress based on a Victorian design would indeed look incongruous if the covered buttons were replaced by a zip. Nonetheless, there are alternatives which a good designer or dressmaker should be able to offer you. Tiny covered buttons are sweet, but unless the dress is a very good fit, they do have a tendency to come undone.

Trimmings of any kind need to be chosen with care and with the whole wedding outfit in mind. Making decisions on trimmings before the dress itself is finalised will only make you look at worst like a Christmas tree and at best as though you are trying to please everyone.

Embroidery and beading on the wedding dress, veil and shoes remain popular, as do other forms of decoration, for example the inclusion of flowers, either real, paper or silk, in the wedding outfit. It is important to remember that while these forms of decoration may be taken directly from fashion history, the quality of the decoration may not equal its original inspiration. Pearl or crystal beading would always have used real pearl and real crystal and commercial contemporary equivalents cannot achieve the same effect. Never allow a beautifully designed and beautifully made dress to be let down by mediocre decoration. It is far better to stay simple.

JEWELLERY

Bridal jewellery is a very personal matter, although a few guidelines would not be out of place.

In general it is best not to mix real with artificial so brides would be well advised to opt for less showy, real jewellery which will not put their wedding and engagement rings into the shade.

Stay simple. To have too many different or conflicting jewels included, whether worn or applied to the outfit can confuse the look. If you are choosing to have pearl beading applied to the dress, stick to pearls, if diamante, stick to diamonds, and if they cannot be real, choose small, rather than large, imitations. The same applies to wearing gold and silver together.

HEADDRESSES

Whether or not they choose to wear a veil, brides will usually wear some sort of decoration in their hair and this does provide a visual balance to the wedding outfit. Headdresses can be made from real or artificial flowers and the style and size must be in proportion to the size of the bride's head and hairstyle. Flowers and greenery can also be used more informally and pinned simply into the hair for a less contrived look.

Over the centuries and across the world, women have decorated their hair and clothing with blossoms, shells, jewels and fabrics and this has prompted styles for wedding headdresses. Family tiaras have an enduring appeal and there is probably something very nice about knowing that a part of your wedding outfit has graced the appearance of brides who have gone before.

Headdresses need to be chosen with the whole outfit in mind and must be appropriate. Circlets can often be too young where a simple band will be better suited, but any choice should always be well and truly tested out beforehand.

SHEPHERDESS, EMPRESS OR TEMPTRESS?
If all the brides in the world were to be put in a test tube over a bunsen burner, and reduced to their essential chemical make-up, it is almost as if three highly different stylistic nuggets would result.

Every bride has a specific and obviously personal self-image of how she will be perceived on her wedding day. Though each girl may give it her own made-up name, experience has taught that bridal attitude as expressed in the great day, and more specifically in the great dress, can be universally pinpointed.

The Shepherdess has an intensely romantic side to her character that is as complicated and embellished as the frill-bedecked frock she chooses to marry in. The Shepherdess remains most people's preconception of a bride. She sees herself as girlish, and fundamentally a child of nature. There are undeniable overtones of Marie Antoinette and her toy farm, yet today's Shepherdess has understood that the key to a relaxed and calm wedding is the acceptance of it as an exceptional, perhaps even theatrical, event.

The Empress is undeniably in charge, not only of her life, which she lives strictly on her own terms, but also of her wedding. As she walks up the aisle she will almost certainly be reflecting with some pride on her negotiating skills and sheer determination that have resulted in the 25% discount granted on the canapés by the caterer. The dress she chooses to express herself may not always be imperial, and may perhaps err somewhat towards high fashion, but it will always be a strong statement.

The Temptress is the dark horse and difficult to categorise. For two thousand years man has never been entirely sure who tempted who, Eve or the Anaconda. Keep a close eye on the Shepherdess or the Empress as either make their grand entrance. Frocks that plunge a little too deep, nails like a lioness fresh from the kill, provide clues to this consummate shape-changer. Of all the categories, the Temptress is most specifically a state of mind rather than dress, though having said that anything a little inappropriate or a touch outré will often lead you to the door of the Temptress' lair!

Having established our corps de ballet, three of the country's leading designers illustrate hypothetical design solutions for three hypothetical brides.

## Zandra Rhodes and the Shepherdess

'The "Shepherdess Bridal Gown" is very loosely eighteenth century in inspiration. The bride wears panniers and bodice in silk organza "Egyptian Stars" print. Wired satin ribbon bows trim the shoulders, waist and elbows and catch up the panniers. She wears a tiered, frilled net underskirt. The panniers and pleating at the neck and sleeve endings are edged with pearls.'

## Jacques Azagury and the Empress

'I find that the most flattering line at the moment is the "Empire line". A jewelled lace bodice teamed with a plain silk georgette and crêpe skirt, gently beaded at the hemline and along the train, disappearing to a trickle of beads towards the bodice.

'Not being cut at the waist the empire line gives added height and an appearance of slimness. An altogether young and glamorous wedding dress.'

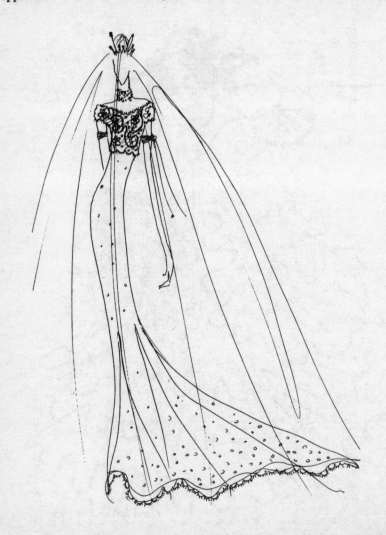

## Vivienne Westwood and the Temptress

'This bride clearly enjoys glamour and uses the situation of her wedding to her own advantage, to indulge her femininity and emphasise her figure. She wears "The Dream Coat" in transparent white lace trimmed with marabou feathers. Her blue fishnet stockings are held up with a garter of flowers. She wears elevated court shoes in white satin, and carries a bouquet of white lilies.'

## THE CIVIL WEDDING BRIDE

Register Office weddings are far less steeped in tradition than those which take place in religious establishments. Consequently, there is much less pressure to conform to the traditional bridal appearance.

Civil brides may wear whatever they like to be married although consideration should be given to the solemnity of the occasion. The Registrar who will marry you is hardly likely to turn up wearing anything shocking or inappropriate and you should really show the same respect in return.

Brides marrying in Register Offices or licensed wedding venues would traditionally wear something smart. Skirts would be considered more appropriate than trousers, but this is a very personal matter. Day-length dresses or suits in any colour, including a bridal shade are perfectly acceptable and would be customary. Plenty of brides marrying in a Register Office or venue do opt for a very obviously bridal appearance wearing everything except the veil and only you will know whether or not you could really consider this to be appropriate to your age, situation and the Register Office in question.

## BRIDAL BEAUTY

If glowing skin, sparkling eyes and healthy hair and nails are important to you as you consider your wedding day style, these cannot be left unaddressed until the week before the wedding.

Few of us are able to devote the time and care we would like to our appearances on a daily basis. It is not just the outward appearance that suffers. Health, too, is often ignored in the pressure to achieve our personal and professional targets. Skin, hair, nails, eyes, in fact every focus of beauty is affected by our state of health, so being healthy, rather than beautiful, for our weddings should be at the centre of our efforts.

Making a decisive move towards a healthier lifestyle often needs a firm reason. There can be no more justifiable reason than a marriage and the start of a whole new life. Set yourself realistic goals which you know you can achieve rather than making plans to lose five stone in a month. Regular exercise and a healthy balanced diet with plenty of fresh fruit and vegetables will be a far better fat reducer than any amount of crash diets and apart from losing weight, you will probably be surprised to find how good you feel. As far as possible, avoid alcohol and cigarettes, they do nothing for beauty.

Sleep is very important. It is during the hours of sleep that our bodies repair the damage we inflict. Educating yourself into a good pattern of sleep before your wedding will greatly help the way you deal with stress and all the inevitable excitement.

There is a great deal of truth in the old saying that a healthy body is a healthy mind. As a method of dealing with stress, exercise is hard to beat. As with any other aspect of your life, it must be approached with equilibrium. There is nothing healthy about someone exhausted through over-exercising.

Healthy hair and nails require regular, not haphazard, attention and the more often they are cut, the faster and stronger they grow. Plan to visit the hairdresser you intend to use for your wedding several months in advance for advice on how to get your hair into the best possible condition for the wedding. If you are going to assist the colour at all, do it now, rather than waiting until closer to the wedding and thereby giving everyone a shock as you suddenly emerge a blonde.

Wedding finery makes such an impact of its own, you need to retain an identity underneath it all. Never be persuaded into choosing make-up or a hairstyle that is different from the way you normally look. Certainly, some styles of dress do require hair to be put up or worn down and these are things you should think about. Weddings can be quite unrealistic enough as it is without your having a serious identity crisis just before you head off for the service.

Make-up for weddings is a matter of personal choice. Most brides prefer a very natural look and many live to regret not actually wearing enough for it to show up in the photographs. Natural make-up needs to be understood and does not refer to the amount that is applied, but to the effect it creates. Professional make-up artists and hairdressers who specialise in wedding work are very helpful in assessing how much, or how little make-up or backcombing and curling a bride is likely to need and will always agree to at least one practice session. Headdresses and veils, hats and tiaras should always be tried out for fit and size by the person with the ultimate responsibility of attaching them on the day.

As you work towards your wedding day and channel your energy and effort into a time in the future, it is important to remember to reward yourself with the odd treat. Facials and massages can be relaxing and good for your circulation as well as your sense of composure. Do not fall into the trap of having either a facial or a massage too close to the wedding. Both can bring impurities in the skin closer to the surface and can cause spots in the short term. They can also make you so relaxed it is impossible to get anything done!

A last word, and this time on the subject of sunbeds. Many brides consider a course of sunbeds before their wedding. Any form of tanning, whether real or artificially gained, can be dangerous and only very stupid people could ever argue that ultraviolet light is actually good for the skin. It is not and damage caused to cell structure is permanent. Do be careful of sunbeds. Nobody needs a tan to be married. Unless the colour of your skin is natural to you, you could look out of place. At your own wedding – imagine!

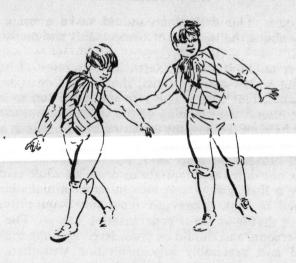

# CHAPTER 2
# The Attendants

The clothing worn by bridesmaids and other attendants is usually the choice of the bride and chosen by her to match or at least reasonably harmonise with her own choice of wedding outfit.

As previously mentioned, the bride and her family are not traditionally expected to pay for the outfits of bridesmaids and other attendants, the costs being met by the parents of smaller children or by the adult attendants themselves. Any bride intending to follow this tradition must give a little thought to who she then does ask to be a bridesmaid and how much they can realistically be expected to afford. There is nothing to stop a bride from offering to include the costs of outfits for her bridesmaids in the general wedding budget, in which case she should make this offer part of the invitation and before any cause is given for embarrassment.

Dresses and accessories for bridesmaids will often be surprisingly costly. Even a very simple dress for a tiny child can be an expensive item and when several attendants are to be dressed, the total bill can easily match the cost of the

bridal gown. This fact alone should make a bride think
seriously about the number of bridesmaids she really wants
or needs.

To have an adult chief bridesmaid, or matron of honour,
depending on her marital status, should be a decision every
bride makes. Not only is it easier and more fun to involve
someone else in the planning of the wedding, and useful to
have her help on the day, the enduring bond between a bride
and her bridesmaid is intensely special. In considering what
the chief bridesmaid is to wear, a bride must consider her
age. It is not only inappropriate to dress an adult as though
she were a little girl, it can also be most humiliating. She
does need to look smart and must not detract from the
bride, but that is as far as generalisation can go. The rest is
purely personal and should be considered with the individual
in mind and preferably in consultation with her. Adult
bridesmaids do not necessarily have to have a dress specially
made for the wedding and will often wear a smart suit or
dress with a hat in the way that they would if they were
simply attending the wedding as any other guest. If they are
dressed to match the bride, they will normally wear a simpler
dress or suit, perhaps in the same fabric or colour, but
designed to flatter their figure.

Little children can normally wear almost anything since they
usually enjoy dressing up and are often too young to know
what is going on anyway. Baby soldiers, sailors or flower
fairies, it doesn't matter so long as the styles chosen for them
to wear are comfortable and have some bearing on the style of
the wedding.

What, if anything, the chief bridesmaid or any others carry
is again a personal matter. If a bride does choose to carry a
bouquet, as most do, her attendants will normally carry similar
but smaller versions. Flower baskets, balls, decorated hoops
and drums are all popular for smaller attendants.

The styling of bridesmaids is one of the areas of a wedding
that offer brides the opportunity to indulge their creative
talents. It is customary for the bride to give each attendant a
small gift, usually a piece of jewellery, to be worn at the
ceremony.

Having young bridesmaids or page boys can greatly add to
the administrative burden of the bride and if there is any
question of her needing to go on a recruitment drive to find

enough under-fives, she might be better advised to do without them. Organising fittings for children whose shape is likely to change beyond all recognition over the course of six months is not all that easy and the greater the number, the more problems likely to arise and take up her valuable time.

# CHAPTER 3

# The Groom, Best Man and Male Members of the Party

It is generally accepted that the traditional male clothing for a wedding is morning dress although the reasons for this are perhaps a little less well understood.

In the past, it was normal for weddings to take place at an earlier stage of the day than is currently the choice of most brides. This is clearly demonstrated by the fact that for a long time, wedding receptions were referred to as wedding breakfasts.

It is a short step of logic to accept that the dress adopted by gentlemen in the morning would be termed 'morning dress' in the way in which clothing for the evening is referred to as 'evening dress'. A gentleman dressing for his daily activities would at one time have started the day off in morning dress regardless of whether he was on his way to his work, his club or indeed a wedding. It is only as a result of the changes which have inevitably simplified our day-to-day lives and consequently, our dress, that gentlemen no longer attire themselves initially in morning dress and change to evening dress after six o'clock, on a daily basis. Diplomatic, Royal and formal social events, however, are a different matter and many still require the attendance of guests in clothing appropriate to the ancient traditions and time of day.

Weddings have always been considered formal social events and the age-old traditions of clothing for both men and women have held fast. If this tradition of etiquette is followed correctly, a gentleman invited to a wedding that is to start later in the day and to be followed by an evening reception would question whether he should, in fact, attend in morning dress or in black tie and may well seek advice from his hosts on this point. No gentleman would ever have considered morning dress to be suitable attire in which to be discovered at an evening party. Quite the contrary, it would have suggested a certain amount of laziness or disorganisation on his part. It is, even now, actually incorrect for a gentleman to arrive at a wedding that is to take place at a late point in the afternoon in morning dress. Being truly correct, however, involves understanding the context in which you will be judged. It would not be correct to be the only person to turn up in evening dress and therefore if the question arises, a gentleman will always seek advice from his hosts.

Contemporary British gentlemen are often the victims of their own inverted snobbery on this point. Since the only formal dress code adopted by many of our European neighbours is black tie, this is usually worn for all formal social occasions including weddings. This has for many years prompted British gentlemen to feel in some way superior in their understanding of the difference between day and evening dress and to look down their noses at what they regard as the uncivilised habits of foreigners. We must wonder how they would feel if it was pointed out to them that by attending an evening wedding in morning dress, it is they and not their European neighbour sitting firmly in his black jacket and bow tie, that have misunderstood the fundamental implications of dress codes!

All this serves to highlight the fact that the contemporary

application of etiquette is not necessarily correct even by those who would be the first to state that their education and upbringing have taught them the difference between good and bad social comportment.

When a man decides to get married, he must also decide whether or not he is going to adopt the dress traditions of centuries before him or opt for a more contemporary style. For most men, this choice will be made between morning dress, black tie or a smart suit. This is a decision he must make after due consultation with his bride. It is wrong to include any reference other than to 'black tie' on a wedding invitation and a travesty itself to put 'morning dress', or worse, 'top hat'. If guests are also expected to attend in a particular style of dress, this fact needs to be diplomatically and verbally communicated. It may well involve the greater number of your guests hiring morning dress or dinner jackets and this is a cost they will incur which you must be aware of and plan to make worth their while in what you arrange for the reception.

For the sake of symmetry, and to make as big an impact as possible, it is usual for all the men in the bridal party to opt for the same dress code. Subtle differences in ties or perhaps waistcoats can be employed to express individuality. The current vogue for accents of colour or exotic patterns in waistcoats, cravats or ties indulge the peacock in any man.

Correct wedding attire for gentlemen used to be even more complicated in reality, according to the formality of the event and whether the wedding was to take place in the town or in the country.

A very formal or town wedding would require the following:

A black tail coat worn with light trousers, a grey or black waistcoat, wing collar, and Ascot tie or 'four-in-hand' (a cravat impossible to tie from scratch – literally requiring four hands and now always bought ready fastened), black socks and shoes, grey suede gloves and a black silk hat. In winter a black or dark grey overcoat would be added. Spats remained a popular addition to this outfit well into the first half of this century.

Only at a less formal or country wedding would a grey coat and matching trousers be worn with a grey hat and gloves. Thankfully, the demands made by weddings upon the wardrobes of gentlemen now are less extreme and a general interpretation of morning dress that would cover any eventuality would consist of:

A black morning coat, grey, black or fawn waistcoat (brocade is currently more popular with grooms), striped black and grey trousers and black socks and shoes. Alternatively, a three piece coat, waistcoat and trouser suit in grey birdseye flannel, often a direct revival of the more formal Edwardian double-breasted style. Hats are rarely actually worn and most of the time end up being carried, so they really could be done without, though many photographers can provide one of the best photographs of the wedding by encouraging all the men present to throw their hats in the air as a background to the newly married couple.

It is customary that all male members of the bridal party, including the ushers, wear a flower in their buttonhole. The groom's flower should traditionally come from the bride's bouquet, though in reality the same florist would do.

To Hire or To Buy

It is not a particularly expensive business to hire morning dress for the odd occasion and if the times when you are likely to wear it are few and far between, it makes more financial sense to do so. This can be achieved with remarkable ease, provided it is done well in advance and will involve little more than a trip to a hire shop of which there are usually plenty in any large town, to be measured and fitted. You will probably pay a small deposit against the sum and collect the clothing a couple of days before it is needed, remembering to return it in good time and complete with all the component parts. Do, however, ensure that plans are made before the groom disappears on honeymoon to return the outfit and retrieve the deposit, a duty best left with the best man.

Nonetheless, there does seem to come a time in everybody's life when all their friends are getting married. If you know that in the course of a year you are getting married and so are a number of your friends and you anticipate wearing morning dress for the majority of these events, it may well be cheaper to actually buy the morning dress. Many hire shops sell off their ex-hire outfits which while in good condition, will be a fraction of the 'new' price. With some research, the required kit can be built up over some years buying an item at a time and hiring the rest until you have the complete set.

## KILTS AND UNIFORMS

Any groom in the armed forces is likely to wish to be married in regimental uniform and his bride would probably insist on this being the case for the colour and ceremony if nothing else. Uniforms and kilts are wonderfully ceremonial and suit the traditions of a wedding extremely well. Regimental uniforms are unlikely to be worn by anyone not fully versed with how they should be worn. Kilts need a little specialist attention unless they themselves form part of a regimental uniform and should certainly only be worn because of some Scots connection. As much etiquette is attached to tartans, kilts and ceremonial Scottish dress as to English peculiarities.

As discussed earlier, the stage management of a wedding requires the male protagonists to be dressed the same. This is particularly relevant with regard to uniforms or kilts, where it is essential that at the very least, the best man and groom sport the same dress. This seemingly trivial point may often have a significant bearing on the choice of the best man. If the groom plans to marry in full regimental outfit, yet his oldest friend's only foray into uniform was with the cub scouts, the basic decision has to be tackled whether friendship is more important than sartorial display.

# The Mothers

One of the fundamental points of wedding etiquette is that neither of the mothers, nor any guest at a wedding should ever choose a white or cream outfit. Not only is it inappropriate for any woman other than the bride or one of her bridesmaids to wear white, these days when the bride is quite likely to have chosen an off-white or pastel shade of dress, having a mother or guest more white than she is will be seen as embarrassing, if not positive upstaging.

Wedding guests, and this includes families, should be as smart, colourful and appropriately dressed as possible. In the past it was traditional for the mothers of the bride and groom to adopt the length of dress chosen by the bride and her attendants. This is now not the case at all and hilarity would no doubt ensue if the mother of any modern bride was to be seen sporting a full length evening dress at her daughter's afternoon wedding.

Wedding mothers should certainly be guided in their choice of outfit by the bride and a certain amount of conferral should be positively encouraged. Two women of obvious importance gracing the same wedding photograph in either identical or clashing shades of peacock blue will almost certainly provoke the odd comment during the reception, if not dominate the speeches. The best policy is for each to pick a colour, known to the other and chosen to fit into whatever colour scheme has been chosen for the bride's appearance, the flowers and reception venue.

Even at relatively informal weddings, it is usual for the mothers of the bride and groom to wear hats and a wedding in fact provides the perfect and relatively rare opportunity to do so. Ladies are not in general supposed to remove their hats during a seated meal at a formal event and wedding guests will usually take their cue in this respect from the behaviour of the mothers. If a hat has been chosen with care, to match an outfit bought for an important occasion such as a wedding, the maximum use and enjoyment of it might as well be made. It is also important to remember that certain religious wedding ceremonies require the female members of the congregation to cover their heads and this is something you may need to pay particular attention to if your mother or your fiancé's mother is not aware of the fact. Marrying into another culture or marrying someone from another culture, or even different social background, however close it may seem, can be the cause of all sorts of misunderstandings and friction so do be sure to remember this if it in any way applies to your situation.

Mothers may, if they choose, wear a corsage of flowers designed to match the bridal flowers and in keeping with their own colour scheme.

# The Ceremony

# The Ceremony

According to the civil law of the United Kingdom, a marriage must be solemnised by an authorised person and in the presence of two witnesses, whether the ceremony is a civil or religious one. The minimum age for marriage is sixteen years, although those under the age of eighteen will require the permission and written consent of a parent or guardian except in Scotland, which accounts for its erstwhile popularity for underage marriages in the earlier part of this century and the notoriety of such places as Gretna Green.

Because the process of marriage and the laws governing what may and may not be done are necessarily complicated, it would be wise to read the following chapters applying to civil as well as religious marriages, since certain points raised are reinforced or changed according to the ceremony which is to take place.

Certain fundamentals apply. Any religious marriage which is to take place must also be recognised by the civil authorities as having been performed in accordance with civil law. Friction between the Church and the State is a fact which dominates much of European history and even today, in France, all couples are required by law to be married in a civil ceremony whether or not they are also intending to have a religious wedding because the Church and the State have never been able to reconcile their differences.

As a member of the majority religion of the United Kingdom, a Church of England Minister solemnising a marriage is accepted to be acting on behalf of both Church and State. In previous times this would have meant that a wedding performed in any other religion, even in other Christian denominations, would require the presence of the local Registrar or someone acting on behalf of the civil authorities. It is easy to imagine just how busy the life of a Registrar would be if he or she was rushing about all over the place, witnessing and recording all religious marriages not performed within the Church of England. Consequently, it is certainly more practical for the civil authorities to license certain individuals other than Church of England ministers, as Marriage Secretaries, responsible for witnessing and recording marriages on behalf of the State. These will be either ministers or particular members of the congregations of other religions. If no person is licensed to act as Registrar on behalf of the State, a Registrar may be required to be present at the ceremony. The permutations of marriage law are most complicated, so any couple not quite sure ought to ask for advice from their minister on this point. The bottom line is that any non-conformist marriage will require certain preliminary civil requirements to be met and notice of the forthcoming marriage will be required to be given at the office of the local Registrar.

# CHAPTER 1
# The Civil Wedding

## 1. The civil wedding in England and Wales

A civil marriage takes place in a Register Office or other venue licensed for the purpose under the authority of the Chief Superintendent Registrar. Until 1994 the law stipulated that in England and Wales a couple could only be married by the Registrar in authority in the district in which one or both of the couple actually lived. Couples were known to go to covert lengths to be married in attractive Register Offices. The Marriage Act 1949 was (finally!) amended by the Marriage Act 1994 and these residency restrictions were lifted, allowing couples to now marry in a civil ceremony in any district.

You may be married in a civil ceremony by either CERTIFICATE or LICENCE. The first step is to visit the office of the Chief Superintendent Registrar in the Town Hall in the district in which you live, where you will be advised on the procedures involved and any specific legal issues applicable to your particular situation. This visit should be made as soon as possible. Even if you are planning to be married in a district other than the one in which either or both of you live, you will still need to give notice at your local Town Hall(s).

MARRIAGE BY SUPERINTENDENT REGISTRAR'S CERTIFICATE

'Giving notice' means visiting the Register Office and filling in a form giving your personal details, the address of where the marriage will take place and signing a declaration stating that there is no legal impediment to the marriage. In the case of minors, the consent of their parents must also be obtained. Notice of the forthcoming marriage is posted on the public notice boards in the Town Hall(s). If the Superintendent Registrar is satisfied with the information given, and no objection to the marriage has been raised, he/she will issue the certificate allowing the marriage to take place twenty-one clear days after notice was given. The certificate allows the couple to be married by appointment at any time within three calendar months from the date of issue. Some very busy Register Offices and Registrars now operate a system whereby couples may make provisional appointments for their weddings up to six months in advance. This does not, of course, affect the legal requirements in any way and the marriage appointment cannot be confirmed until the certificate has been issued.

MARRIAGE BY SUPERINTENDENT REGISTRAR'S LICENCE
This is the 'fast track'. Notice is given at the Register Office and one clear day must elapse before the licence is issued allowing the marriage to take place. Although legally only one partner needs to give notice when doing so by licence, it is helpful if both parties can attend to discuss the arrangements. Marriage by licence is generally chosen by couples who wish to be married as soon as possible rather than wait the twenty-one days necessary for the issue of a certificate, as well as those who would prefer the confidentiality of this method, which does not require the posting of public notices. Marriage by licence is a little more expensive than marriage by certificate.

DIVORCEES AND SECOND MARRIAGES IN ENGLAND AND WALES
A divorced person may be married in a civil ceremony provided that he or she can fulfil the legal requirements. A 'Decree Nisi' will be granted once a divorce agreement is reached, but a 'Decree Absolute' is required before a further marriage of either party may take place. The 'Decree Absolute' must be applied for and this application may not be made before six weeks and one day have elapsed from the granting of the 'Decree Nisi'.

## 2. The civil wedding in Scotland
There are no residential requirements for marriages which take place in Scotland. A couple wishing to be married, either by the Registrar or by a registered celebrant (religious minister), must give notice at the office of the Superintendent Registrar in whose district the marriage is to take place. Notice of the forthcoming marriage is posted on the public notice boards and if, after fifteen clear days, no objections are raised, the Superintendent Registrar will issue a marriage schedule. If the marriage is to take place in the office of the Registrar, this marriage schedule is kept there until the wedding. If the marriage is to be celebrated in a religious ceremony, the marriage schedule is sent to the minister who will officiate at the ceremony.

## Divorcees and Second Marriages in Scotland

According to Scottish marriage law, the decree of divorce is 'absolute' from the time the divorce is granted and the parties are free to marry again immediately. The granting of the marriage schedule may, however, take a little longer.

## What Happens at a Civil Wedding?

Having booked an appointment for the marriage and assured themselves that the necessary certificate(s), licence or schedule has been issued, the bride and groom arrive at the Register Office either together or separately and normally with a group of friends and family. Registrars are usually very busy and will not take kindly to couples who do not arrive in good time. Some Register Offices have two or more rooms in which marriages can take place according to the number of guests expected, although few are really big enough to accommodate more than 100 guests, so licensed venues might offer more scope for larger numbers.

Whether at a Register Office or a licensed venue, the Registrar will wish to have a brief meeting in private with the bride and groom a few minutes before the appointed time, to assure him/herself that all is in order. At this point, the guests usually take their seats and wait for the couple to enter the room with the Registrar.

It is an interesting point of law that marriages must be solemnised in premises with open doors allowing the public unfettered access to witness the marriage and make objections prior to or during the ceremony. However modern we might think we have become, echoes of the laws of the 1800s designed to prevent bigamous marriage still ring today.

Civil weddings have been known in the past to be short and to the point, although they have never been without ceremony. Although not common knowledge, music and words can be included in the ceremony and certainly, in a licensed venue, there is no reason why the room cannot be as fully decorated as anyone would wish. Consultation with and approval from the Registrar conducting the marriage must always be sought.

Having been declared husband and wife, the couple then sign the register, as do their two witnesses and the Registrar. Couples wishing to have photographs or a video taken during the ceremony must seek permission from the Registrar in advance, since this is at his/her discretion.

Once the marriage has taken place and the required signatures have been given, the bride and groom and their guests will normally leave the Register Office promptly, perhaps having some photographs taken outside if there is a suitable location. In a licensed venue, it would be normal for the assembled group to then move in to another room for the Reception.

Fees are payable to the Superintendent Registrar for the solemnisation of marriages and the issue of certificates and licences. These fees are set by the Treasury to keep in line with inflation, so are usually subject to a small increase from the 1st April each year.

# CHAPTER 2
# The Church of England Wedding

A parish priest in the Church of England has a duty to solemnise marriages of parishioners on request, or to make the church available to another clergyman for this purpose. This is at his discretion if either party has been previously married and still has a surviving spouse.

Couples may be married on any day of the week, between the hours of 8 a.m. and 6 p.m. and discussion will usually arise over the question of whether at least one of the couple has been baptised.

Couples may be married by banns, by common (or ordinary) or special licence.

## Marriage by Banns
The minister will 'read the banns' (or announce the forthcoming marriage) to the congregation during Sunday Service over three successive Sundays. Banns are required to be read in the parish churches of both parties, as well as the church in which the wedding is to take place if neither of these. Once the banns have been read in this manner, the marriage may take place at any time within three calendar months. If the marriage does not take place during this period, the banns are invalid and must be re-read in the same manner before the marriage can take place.

## Marriage by Common or Ordinary Licence
A common licence is granted by the Surrogate for the Bishop of the Diocese in which the marriage is to take place. The ordinary licence allows a couple to be married without the reading of banns. The wedding must take place in the parish church or usual place of worship of one of the couple and one party is required to be resident in or to be on the electoral register of the parish for a minimum of fifteen days before the licence will be granted.

One of the parties is required to collect the licence in person and sign a declaration, on oath, stating that there is no legal impediment to the marriage and that he or she has fulfilled the residential requirements. The licence is then given to the officiating minister, who may perform the ceremony immediately, or within three months from its date of issue. If, after this period the marriage has not taken place, another licence must be applied for.

## MARRIAGE BY SPECIAL LICENCE

In general terms, a special licence allows marriages to take place in unusual situations. This can apply to a marriage taking place in a church other than the parish churches of the couple or at a time of day outside the normally permitted hours or, in an emergency situation, for example if one partner is ill or unable to be married in the normal fashion. The granting of a special licence will depend upon the support of the minister who will marry the couple and their providing good reasons for why the marriage should take place outside their normal parishes and will normally require the written consent of the parents of the couple. The special licence is issued by the Faculty Office, by the Archbishop of Canterbury. In the same way as an ordinary licence, one of the couple is required to collect the special licence in person and sign a declaration, on oath, stating that there is no legal impediment to the marriage. The special licence having been issued, the marriage may take place within three months. If the marriage does not take place during this period, the special licence becomes invalid and another must be applied for.

Couples planning to marry within the Church of England are normally required to accept pre-nuptial counselling from the minister who will marry them, which will usually take the form of at least three meetings to discuss the implications of the commitment they are making to one another and to go through details of the ceremony. When the wedding date is in sight, an appointment will be made for a rehearsal which the bride and groom must both attend, usually with their families and attendants.

It must be stressed that these are necessarily brief and broad outlines of the legalities and requirements for marriages within the Church of England and couples should always be advised to make contact with the minister they hope will marry them at the earliest opportunity.

WHAT HAPPENS AT A CHURCH OF ENGLAND WEDDING?
Guests will arrive in advance of the two families and will be welcomed by the ushers. The groom and his best man normally arrive half an hour before the ceremony. The bride's mother arrives at the church with the bridesmaids, five minutes or so before the bride arrives, accompanied by her father, or whoever is 'giving her away'. The groom's parents and then the bride's mother are escorted to their seats in the front pews of the church by the chief usher, the family of the bride being seated on the left and the family of the groom seated on the right.

The bride takes her father's right arm and is escorted down the aisle to meet the groom, who waits with his best man in the first pew on the right of the church, facing the altar and who now turns to welcome his bride. The wording of the ceremony is such that the bride is required to provide somebody to give her away. It is definitely worth pointing out that a bride does not have to be given away by her father or even another male relative or friend. It is quite acceptable for her to be escorted down the aisle by her mother, sister or another close female friend. In fact, this was common in previous decades when so many fathers, brothers and uncles were killed in two World Wars. The bride is followed by her bridesmaids in procession and she normally chooses a piece of music for her 'processional'. The minister will welcome the standing congregation and the ceremony will begin.

During the marriage, the bridesmaids remain standing behind the bride and groom, unless they are too little to be trusted and the bride will turn and hand her bouquet to the chief bridesmaid so that her hands are free to receive the wedding ring. Once the bride's father (or other relative) has indicated his consent to the marriage in answer to the minister's 'Who gives this woman to be married to this man?', by passing the bride's right hand to the minister, he takes his seat in the front pew on the left and the couple then exchange vows.

A great deal of emphasis is often placed on whether a bride chooses to 'obey' her husband or chooses instead, the more modern promise, which the groom would then also make in response, to 'love, honour and cherish'. Considering that she has accepted the bridal role and is quite likely to be wearing the full wedding dress and veil, it is rather an incongruous moment to place too much emphasis on interpretations of equality.

When the couple have exchanged promises, the ring is blessed and the bride receives her ring from the groom. She may also give him a ring. The couple are pronounced to be husband and wife.

Hymns are usually sung before and after the marriage and the couple will sign the register either after having made their promises and been pronounced man and wife or at the end of the ceremony, following prayers. More contemporary couples choose to sign the register in the main body of the church now rather than to disappear from the eyes of guests into the vestry. Two witnesses and the minister will also put their signatures to the church register and the marriage certificate, which is given to the bride. Brides will always sign in their maiden names.

At the end of the ceremony, the newly married couple will leave the church, the bride on the groom's left arm, followed by their attendants, families and guests. The parents of the couple are usually cross-matched and the best man will normally escort the chief bridesmaid. Again, the bride will usually choose a piece of music for the 'recessional' as well as others which could have been played or sung by a choir at various points during the ceremony and signing of the register. Not all ministers give a formal address at a wedding, but two readings are normally given by members of the families or friends of the couple and some time will always be given for prayer.

DIVORCEES AND SECOND MARRIAGES IN THE CHURCH OF ENGLAND

Many clergymen in the Church of England will not solemnise the marriages of parties who have been previously married and divorced if the previous spouse is surviving, unless the circumstances are exceptional. Most, however, will perform a service of blessing (formally known as a Service of Prayer and Dedication) following a civil marriage of a divorcée. The exact content and style of a blessing is very much at the discretion of the minister and couples should seek advice. At a blessing, the couple normally walk down the aisle together as the congregation sings the first hymn and the bride is not given away in the same way as she is during a wedding ceremony, although some ministers will, at their discretion, permit the bride to be escorted to join the groom, particularly if she has never been

married. The couple do, however, publicly confirm the promises they will have already made to each other at the civil
ceremony, this time in the presence of the minister and
congregation.

# CHAPTER 3
# The Church of
# Scotland Wedding

The Church of Scotland marriage ceremony is very similar in style and content to the ceremony performed in the Church of England. The vows the couple exchange are slightly different and the blessing of rings is not usual.

The most significant difference between the Scottish and Anglican Churches regarding marriage concerns the remarriage of divorcées. Ministers in the Church of Scotland will be more likely to agree to solemnise second marriages for divorced persons. It must be stressed, however, that this is by no means a foregone conclusion and couples cannot necessarily expect this to be the case in their particular situation and they would therefore be strongly advised to discuss the matter personally with their minister. By contrast to the Church of England, the Church of Scotland and Scottish law allows couples to be married anywhere, in or outside a building, religious or not, provided that the ceremony is conducted by an authorised minister.

## CHAPTER 4
# The Roman Catholic Wedding

The Roman Catholic wedding ceremony has two forms – with or without mass. Roman Catholic weddings involve the exchange of marriage vows and a special blessing after which mass may be celebrated.

Unlike his Anglican colleagues, a Roman Catholic priest does not act on behalf of the State, so a couple planning to be married in the Roman Catholic Church must also apply to the Civil Authorities for a certificate or licence.

## 1. Mixed marriages

In the Roman Catholic Church, a 'mixed' marriage is one between a Catholic and a non-Catholic. For a mixed marriage to take place, either in a Catholic or Church of England church, a dispensation is required and must be applied for by the parish priest of the practising Catholic. Ministers from both religions may be present and assist at the ceremony although the Church of England marriage service must be followed in a Church of England church and vice versa.

Couples wishing to be married in the Roman Catholic Church will normally be required to accept six months pre-marital counselling, either from the priest who will marry them or in a group with others in a similar situation. This counselling will prompt discussion on all the various areas of responsibility within marriage from the financial considerations to the more personal. In the past, mass could only be celebrated as part of a morning wedding. This is no longer the case. If mass is celebrated, the couple and their families and all other Catholics present will receive communion. The bride and groom are expected to fast for one hour before their wedding is due to take place.

### What Happens at a Catholic Wedding?

The bride is escorted by her father to join the groom, as he stands on the right at the front of the church, after which he leaves her and joins his own wife in the first pew on the left-hand side.

The bride and groom then proceed to the steps of the sanctuary, where the priest is standing and the marriage ceremony takes place there. The chief bridesmaid stands on the bride's left, the best man on the groom's right. Other bridesmaids divide to alternate sides, towards the altar. After the ceremony, the attendants follow the couple down the aisle in the recessional.

During the marriage, the couple exchange vows, led by the priest after which he will sprinkle them with holy water and bless the rings. Taking the ring he will give to his bride, the groom places it on the thumb of her left hand, saying, 'In the name of the Father'. Transferring it to her index finger, he continues, 'and of the Son', moves it to the next finger 'and of the Holy Spirit' and so ending up with the third finger of the left hand on to which he slips it saying, finally, 'Amen'. He will then receive his ring from the bride in the same way.

Once the marriage vows and the rings have been exchanged and blessed, the ceremony will finish with prayers. If a nuptial mass is involved, the attendants leave the bride and groom in the sanctuary to receive Holy Communion, taking their places in the first pews on either side of the church. If they are also Catholics, they will receive communion with the families of the couple.

The relationship between the State and the Roman Catholic Church in England has never been an easy one since the time of the Reformation. In the past, when a Roman Catholic marriage had taken place, the civil authorities insisted that a civil declaration was also made, usually taking place in the Sacristy. Now, however, this declaration is no longer necessary, provided a Registrar or other registered person is present to record the event for the civil authorities and witness the signatures of the bride and groom and their chosen witnesses in the church's register. This registered person is usually the parish priest or a parishioner.

## 2. Second marriages

In the Catholic Church, second marriages may only take place if the partner(s) in question have been widowed or if the preceding marriage has been annulled. Second marriages follow the same service, although, dependent upon the age of the couple in question, mention of children from the marriage may not be made.

Couples wishing to be married in the Catholic Church who would like further advice on the attitude of the Church and its teaching on marriage might like to contact The Catholic Truth Society. A recommended text for anyone considering a Catholic marriage is 'Faith in Marriage', by Peter Knott SJ. The Catholic Truth Society can be contacted at 39 Eccleston Square, London SW1.

# CHAPTER 5
# The Jewish Wedding

According to the civil laws of the United Kingdom, a Jewish marriage may be solemnised in any building and at any time of the day, provided the couple in question have obtained and produced the necessary legal document (certificate for marriage) from the Registrar in the district, allowing the ceremony to take place either by certificate or licence (see Chapter 1).

Some couples will be married in a civil ceremony performed by the Registrar before their religious marriage in which case the Certificate *of* Marriage (not the certificate *for* marriage) they are given by the Registrar must be produced.

A great number of Jewish weddings are solemnised in an Orthodox synagogue under the authority of the Chief Rabbi or in a Progressive (Reform or Liberal) synagogue, where the civil authority appoints a Marriage Secretary who is responsible to the Government Offices. The authorisation of the Chief Rabbi or Marriage Secretary must be given for the marriage to take place and he may only give this authorisation if the requirements of civil law have been met. He is also responsible for ensuring that the requirements of Jewish religious law have been fulfilled.

For a couple to marry in the Jewish faith, both the bride and groom must be Jews. For a marriage to be solemnised where only one partner is Jewish, the other partner must undertake a formal conversion which involves demanding instruction and examination. The conversion must be completed before the wedding can take place. When a licence for a marriage in the Jewish community is granted, the groom must be a member of the synagogue in which the wedding is to take place and the Registrar will demand proof of such membership.

Jewish weddings may not be solemnised at any time on the Sabbath, which lasts from sunset on Friday until sunset on Saturday, as this is a Holy time for prayer. Jewish festivals and certain other specific days are also prohibited. Most Jewish weddings take place on Sundays.

On the Sabbath (or Saturday) preceding the wedding day,

the bridegroom and his father and the father of the bride and other close relatives of the couple will normally attend divine service in the synagogue in which the wedding is to take place. The bridegroom will often be invited to read a lesson from the Scroll of Law or Pentateuch.

Jewish law suggests that an orthodox bride and groom should fast on their wedding day and offer special prayers in order to enter their new life together cleansed of past sins and strengthened in their faith. The bride will normally wear a veil, the bridegroom and all other men present must wear hats, whether the synagogue is orthodox or progressive. In Orthodox synagogues, women also should have their heads covered and even in Progressive synagogues, one should check on individual practices.

## WHAT HAPPENS AT A JEWISH WEDDING?

The groom will arrive at the synagogue with his father and best man who form his escort and will 'give him away' in marriage and meet up with the bride's father or whoever is 'giving her away'. They sit together in the most prominent pew in the synagogue. When the bride arrives, the groom is escorted under the chuppah. The male members of the bridal party then leave the synagogue to escort the ladies inside. The bride is led in on the arm of her father and is followed in procession by the bridesmaids and the mothers of the couple. The groom's mother will be escorted by her husband, the bride's mother by a son or other male relative, since her husband is escorting their daughter. The bride stands to the right of the groom, under the canopy, the bridesmaids behind the couple. Traditionally, the women in the procession stand at the side of the bride and the men at the side of the groom, although in Progressive synagogues, the men and women are not divided but stand together on respective sides of the couple. The bridal party under the canopy faces the Ark, which is at the eastern side of the synagogue, with the minister or ministers standing in between and facing them. There are variants to these customs and many synagogues will have a rehearsal of some sort.

The canopy or chuppah is usually rectangular, made of silk or velvet and supported by poles. Chuppahs vary in style and are often very ancient and beautiful. The marriage ceremony is performed under the chuppah, which is often

beautifully decorated with flowers, symbolic of the future
home of the bridal couple, its delicate frailty reminding them
that security in marriage and life depends upon divine
guidance and help. Not all synagogues have a chuppah, in
which case a shawl or Tallit, used normally for prayer may be
used instead, held at each corner by a man and above the
heads of the bride and groom. The Jewish marriage ceremony requires the marriage to be solemnised in the presence of at least ten adult male witnesses, known collectively
as a minyan, although in Progressive synagogues a minyan
may not be insisted on, particularly if the wedding is a
second, or very small, wedding.

The Jewish marriage ceremony opens when a blessing from
the Psalms is given by the minister, sometimes assisted by the
choir. A further Psalm is chanted and the minister gives an
address to the bride and groom, followed by a betrothal
blessing. The bride and groom will then normally declare their
vows to each other in answer to questions posed by the
minister. The groom places a ring on the second finger of the
bride's right hand and declares to her 'Behold, thou art
consecrated unto me by this ring according to the Law of
Moses and of Israel.' In so doing, the marriage is witnessed
and consecrated. In reform or liberal synagogues, the bride
will often give a ring to her husband as well. The marriage
contract, or Ketubah, is then read in both Aramaic and
English.

Following the marriage, the minister or a cantor will chant
a series of benedictions, blessing the couple, the world in
which they live and the Jewish faith. A glass will then be
placed at the feet of the bridegroom for him to stamp on and
break. The glass represents the frail nature of our existence
and the care that needs to be taken to protect the union that
the couple have now entered into. Tradition teaches that the
glass is also broken as a reminder of the destruction of
Jerusalem. Some Liberal synagogues have abandoned the
breaking of the glass, viewing it as something of a medieval
superstition.

The end of the ceremony is signified by the minister, who
pronounces 'The Lord bless you and keep you, the Lord make
His face to shine upon you and be gracious unto you, the Lord
lift up His countenance upon you and give you peace.' Other
Psalms may be introduced and sung during the service and

wedding marches are usually used for the bride's procession and the couple's recessional.

Unless the couple have already had a civil marriage at which they would have signed the register and fulfilled the legal requirements, they now do so, in the register of the synagogue, as do two witnesses and these signatures are countersigned by the synagogue's authorised Secretary for Marriages and usually also by the officiating minister.

When a Jewish marriage is to take place, it is customary for the couple to visit the Rabbi for pre-marital counselling. The Rabbi may refer them to an expert counsellor.

## SECOND MARRIAGES IN THE JEWISH FAITH

If a second marriage is to take place, the couple will be required to visit the Rabbi since there are often legal issues to be resolved. Beyond the Decree Absolute, which the civil law of the United Kingdom requires to permit the marriage, Jewish religious law requires that a Jewish bill of divorce has been issued to the partner who has been previously married. Most Progressive synagogues today also make this a stipulation. This may involve an appointment with the Beth Din (Rabbinical Court) which also exists in the Progressive Movement.

There are other issues which may arise in second marriages, such as adoption, which would also need advice regarding Jewish Law governing such situations.

Wherever problems are anticipated, a bride and groom should call upon the office of the Chief Rabbi for Orthodox Jews or the Progressive authorities which the Rabbi of a Reform or Liberal synagogue will recommend.

In Judaism, a marriage is a joyful occasion and emphasis on a happy family life has always been at the heart of the Jewish tradition.

Regardless of where, how and by whom your marriage is to be solemnised, you must make it your concern to discuss matters arising at the earliest opportunity. Both the civil and religious authorities are experienced in the legal and often personal problems contemporary couples encounter in connection with their marriages and will be happy to explain the implications of any processes or requirements which might apply.

For more information for legal requirements for marriage in the UK contact:

England and Wales – The General Register Office 0171 242 0262

Scotland – The General Register Office 0131 334 0380

Northern Ireland – The General Register Office 0232 235211

Eire – The General Register Office 00 353 1 711000

SECTION SIX

# The Countdown

The last few weeks of wedding planning can be as frustrating as the first. The major decisions have been made, the invitations sent and replies received, final fittings are over and so the waiting game begins. All of a sudden it seems as though there is nothing left to do but count the days away.

Having spent many months in a flurry of activity, thinking that all the work will never be done, this new phase is bound to stir up feelings of unease. How can it possibly be finished? What should I be doing now? Have I forgotten anything? With so much time, effort and, not least, money invested in the wedding, what can you do to make sure that it all goes according to plan?

It is during this time that brides are most likely to fall victim to nerves and panic and it is important to realise that you must find constructive ways to pass the last hurdle.

The countdown period is the ideal time to check, recheck and confirm with the army of professionals and helpers involved in your wedding.

# CHAPTER 1
# Confirming with Suppliers

Any contractor depends on good communication between himself and the client to do a good job. If the information he or she receives is not complete and accurate, the chances are that some disappointment will result. So many wedding factors remain variables until almost the last moment and as you will by now have understood, the final outcome can change accordingly.

Even with the best will and the best attention in the world, information can be misheard, misread or forgotten. It must now be your concern to spend some time going over plans for the wedding and making sure that everyone involved knows as much as they possibly can.

The following questions do not represent a definitive list, which would be impossible to provide. They are merely a selective sampling of the sort of things you should be asking yourself.

1. Have your numbers changed? If so, your caterer or hotel will need to know to be able to order the right amount of equipment and number of staff as well as food quantities.
2. Does the change in numbers mean that you will need one extra or one less table centre at the reception? If so, you need to tell your florist.
3. Does the change in numbers mean that you might need a slightly larger marquee, or could you even get away with a smaller one?
4. Have you clearly confirmed the timings of the day with all your suppliers? Have you provided itineraries of the events for each and everyone concerned? Does the florist know where to deliver the buttonholes? Have you let him or her know when he or she can return to the venue after the wedding and retrieve baskets and pedestals etc. and tidy up the debris from flowers?
5. If you are supplying your own wines, have you thought about ice to chill them? Who is to be responsible for chilling the wine? Are you also expected to supply ice buckets for the wine?

6. Do all suppliers have full addresses and telephone numbers for the various places they might need to find? Do they have a contact telephone number for you, wherever you might be in the last few days before the wedding? Do they have maps? Have you thought about access routes for heavy lorries and vans? Marquee trucks and catering vans can find it difficult to get down little country lanes and across fields. Have you considered where and how they are to park, at the church or synagogue and at the reception venue?

7. Are you involving any entertainers or musicians in your wedding? If so, what will they eat and drink and does your caterer know how many he or she will need to feed and what sort of price you will be prepared to pay for this? Is there somewhere for musicians and staff to change and leave their things securely?

8. Have all necessary deposits been paid? Quotations remain quotations until they are confirmed in writing or a deposit is paid. Have any changes or verbally agreed arrangements with suppliers affected the final price of any items? If so, get everything in writing.

9. Rubbish removal and security – have you given adequate thought to these areas and come to a solution?

10. Have you made a play list of songs you would like to hear or dance to at the reception?

11. Have you sorted out the list of group photographs you would like taken and sent this list to the photographer? Does he or she know if he is supposed to visit you or the groom in the morning of the wedding day and if so, does he or she know where to find you both? Have you discussed whether or not you would like some black and white photography? If he or she cannot stay late at the reception, have you thought about who might be able to take some photographs later on?

12. Is the cake finalised and if so, who is responsible for taking it to the reception and assembling it? Have you asked for a cake table and who is to decorate it? Have you booked a cakestand and knife? Do you have a nice cloth for the cake table at home or does this need to be hired?

13. If you are having a seated meal, have you finalised the seating plan?

# CHAPTER 2
# Assessing the Final Cost

Attentive though you will have been to your initial wedding budget, these variable factors can make a considerable difference when they are finalised. Excitement and expectation can sometimes push the budget limit further and further away from its original settings as in anticipation of the wonderful day yet to be had, certain extra extravagances are somehow allowed. However wonderful a wedding is, families often find the cost harder to justify in retrospect which is why it is even more important not to find yourself with a nasty shock. Finding out that you are way over budget before the wedding means that you can still do something about it. You could opt for sparkling wine instead of champagne or drop the number of canapés slightly. You might decide to do without that extra pedestal arrangement of beautiful but expensive lilies. Finding out that you are over budget after the wedding will just be depressing.

This is now a good moment to prune your wedding file and rid yourself of all the unnecessary paperwork. You are bound to have a certain sense of achievement in doing this.

Having assessed the final cost of your dreams, you must work out a payment schedule to be sure of having the cash/cheque for the right people at the right time. Different suppliers are likely to ask for different percentages at different times according to their business. You will make life far simpler for yourself if you know exactly when money will be needed. It is also more polite and diplomatic to warn parents and in-laws of any costs they are likely to have to meet. Your father is not going to be best pleased if, half-way to the church, you suddenly remember that you were supposed to take a cheque for the best man to give to the groom to pay the minister. If, having paid your deposits, certain suppliers give you a degree of credit on the balance, try to remember to plan ahead. When the time comes around you may be away on your honeymoon. If a supplier of anything has pulled out all the stops to give you a super wedding, it is neither well-mannered nor kind not to pay them on time, or as agreed.

# CHAPTER 3
# Confirming with Families and the Team

If you have instituted a well-structured system of contingency planning meetings with your wedding team, they will be well-used to receiving your summons. If you have not, this is the time you absolutely must insist on at least one.

No bride should ever be made to feel that she alone has to remember what everyone else is supposed to be doing. Your team may well have absorbed a great deal of information to date on their duties and responsibilities and may have come to better understand what you are expecting from them, but successful weddings do depend on each person knowing how they fit into the larger and more general scheme of things.

Arrange a date, not too far from the wedding but before the common sense of your argument gets lost in the excitement. Insist that all members of the team are present. Make a very organised professional list of things to be discussed with reference to each individual and make sure they take it away and study it. In the process you may well be made to feel akin to a schoolmistress, but you will not regret it. Insist on revision. Make a second list of any points you know need to be discussed or responsibility apportioned to achieve certain elusive goals. It really does not matter who does them so long as they are done. The chief bridesmaid can perfectly well pick up suits for the groom and best man if she has more free time than either of them. Logic has to prevail. Make sure that everyone present has and keeps a copy of the itinerary.

# The Hen and Stag Parties

## 1. Stag parties

Stag parties are an accepted feature of the modern wedding. They involve male friends and relatives of the groom and often of the bride as well, getting together and putting on a night of revelry as a farewell to the groom's freedom of bachelorhood.

A clue to the origin of stag parties can be found in German wedding traditions. The night before a wedding was to take place, a rowdy all-night party, known as a 'Polterabend' would be planned at which guests would be encouraged to make as much noise as possible to drive away ghosts and malign spirits.

Stag parties are almost always male-only affairs. This fact seems to explain the notorious excesses and often scandalous events which typically take place. It seems as though when the cat is away the mice will well and truly play.

The organisation of the stag party is the traditional responsibility of the best man. The sequence of anticipated events is usually kept secret from the groom in order to maximise his surprise and enjoyment. How enjoyable any stag party really is will depend on the appropriateness of planned festivities. The best man's duty is to ensure that the groom arrives at and leaves his stag party, not only in one piece but with all his previous faculties intact. Finding himself alone and in a different country without any trousers cannot possibly be a source of amusement to a groom busy with wedding arrangements and attentions to his future wife.

In the past, stag parties would often have taken place the night before the wedding. Nowadays it is far more common for it to be arranged for the weekend or two weekends before. Making binding promises to someone you can hardly recognise through the mist of a hangover shows little or no respect for the effort that everyone will have put into the wedding, least of all for the bride.

Stag parties vary according to the tastes and financial circumstances of those involved and the groom is rarely expected to pay for anything himself. In essence, they should be enjoyable, affordable and only slightly raucous.

## 2. Hen parties

There is no reason why a bride, like her groom, may not spend an evening with close friends as a farewell to her life as a single lady and this has become every bit as much of an established tradition. Hen parties have absorbed the American custom of a 'bridal shower' at which friends of the bride would gather, each bringing a small personal gift for the bride, often along a joint, agreed theme.

As the best man organises arrangements for the groom, so the chief bridesmaid will normally assume responsibility for planning and organising the hen party. A hen party can take the form of a day spent together or a supper party at home or in a restaurant, or a combination of the two. The choice of what to do, where to go and how expensive it is to be should be made with consideration to those involved. The bride, like the groom, is rarely expected to pay for anything herself.

Although it cannot be assumed, particularly of late with the current interest in theatrical displays of muscular prowess set to music, women are generally less given to inappropriate excess at hen parties than their partners at the male equivalent. The chief bridesmaid is as responsible for the welfare of the bride as the best man is for the groom.

## 3. Joint parties

Brides and grooms do not always look forward to the stag and hen parties. They may well share friends of both sexes and prefer not to be steamrollered into accepting what could be seen as enforced rather than natural merriment. In the unusual but possible event of the best man being a woman, the implications of her organising a stag party just for male friends of the groom would be more than a little confusing. The simple answer is to plan a relaxed, joint supper or drinks party somewhere together, with all their friends, male and female. This will be particularly nice for couples who have not had any form of previous engagement celebration, since it does give the couple the chance to enjoy the idea of the forthcoming marriage in informal, uncontrived circumstances.

# CHAPTER 5

# Receiving Line and Wedding Speeches

It may not have escaped your notice that no mention has so far been made of the order or content of wedding speeches or the traditional order for a receiving line. This is specifically to ensure that as you now recap on all of what you must remember, you get the information you need at the right time and in turn relay it to others.

Any member of the families of the bride and groom and their wedding team may speak at the reception if they so wish, provided the bride and groom consent. Wedding speeches are the public welcoming of the guests and offer the chance to express all the glorious sentiments so much at the forefront of our minds at a wedding.

The customary order of speeches is as follows

1. Bride's father
2. Groom
3. Best man

The word 'customary' is chosen with care. In the past it has been quite normal for brides to speak at their weddings on their own behalf, in addition to or in place of their fathers. At various points it has also been quite normal for chief bridesmaids and brides' mothers to give a speech, as is the case for the father of the groom. It is clearly sensible for those with the ability to give the speeches. No bride should ever feel that she is not entitled to welcome the guests herself. Getting married does not mean that you are expected to suddenly lose your voice. If a bride wishes to give a speech at her own wedding, it would be appropriate for her to do this right at the beginning, before anyone else.

## 1. The traditional order for the receiving line
As guests approach the line, they will be received by the bridal party in the following order:

The bride's mother
The groom's father
The groom's mother
The bride's father
The bride
The groom
The chief bridesmaid
The best man

This order does make logical sense. It means that any guest approaching who is not known to one family can be immediately introduced by a representative of the family they do know well. The receiving line does not have to be formal or regimented and families can quite well simply stand together in a group to welcome guests if they prefer.

## 2. The bride's father's speech

The father of the bride will usually enjoy the opportunity to command the attention of all the guests he is quite likely to have spent a great deal of money entertaining. As a general rule, he will dwell on the following points:

● How nice it is to see so many friends present;
● How proud he is of his daughter and her choice of husband;
● How welcome his new son-in-law is as a part of his family.

He may also relate a few nostalgic stories about his daughter during her childhood and teenage years. It is not appropriate for the bride's father to cause her or the groom any embarrassment. He will finish by asking the assembled guests to raise their glasses to 'The bride and groom'.

## 3. The groom's speech

A groom is not expected by tradition to speak for long or to be particularly amusing. The assumption is that he is more than a little emotional and he therefore gets off lightly.

Upon standing, he will courteously thank the bride's father for his toast to himself and his 'wife' – the mere mention of the word should bring applause from the audience and fortify his spirits a little. He will then launch into the list of people it is his duty to thank.

- The guests who have come from far and wide to be with them on their special day – he might mention the furthest points of the compass to add emphasis.
- The bride's parents (if applicable) for the wonderful reception they have generously provided. Even if the bride's family have not incurred the costs of the wedding alone, it would still be seemly to thank them at an early point.
- His own parents for the love and support they have shown him over all the years.
- (He may at this point present a gift or bouquet of flowers to his own and the bride's mother.)
- His best man for his invaluable help and support.
- His wife, for marrying him and making him extremely happy and for looking so beautiful.
- The groom should propose a toast to 'absent friends', reminding the guests that not everyone will have been able to come and that the absentees are in his thoughts.
- Finally, he will thank the bridesmaids for the part they have played and propose a final toast to 'The bridesmaids'.

## 4. The best man's speech

The best man has the hardest job of all in terms of speeches, since he is allowed and therefore expected to show a certain licence to portray the groom in an amusing light. Not all best men are gifted speakers and many dread the moment that eyes and ears will be upon them. At the end of the day, the important thing to remember about wedding speeches is the sincerity that is expressed rather than the words used.

The first duty the best man has to perform in his speech is to thank the groom for his kind words and toast to the bridesmaids on their behalf. To help him settle a little and overcome his nerves, he will then use the opportunity to read out any telemessage or cards which might have arrived that day from absent friends. Once· this has been accomplished, it is very much a question of personal choice. It is perfectly acceptable for the best man to recount various monumental or memorable events he has shared with the groom, even the slightly racy ones. He will usually talk about the bride and what a very appropriate couple she and the groom make. He may well recall his first (favourable of course) impressions of the bride and the positive effect she has had on the groom. The best man's summing up is a final toast to 'The bride and groom – Mr and Mrs . . .'. He will then announce the fact that they will cut the wedding cake, which gives the audience a chance to get their cameras ready.

Wedding speeches should always be kept reasonably short and to the point. Protracted speeches can become boring and lose impact unless the speaker is extremely gifted. Wedding speakers should plan to talk for no more than ten minutes each, fifteen at an absolute maximum. Do remember to make this point during your contingency planning meetings. The sight of a bride embarrassed by anyone's inappropriate or boring speech is a sad one.

You should also bear in mind that while these synopses represent what is traditional and customary, only you will know what sort of speeches will fit your wedding.

# CHAPTER 6
# Seating Plans

If you are having a seated meal at your reception, it is always better to organise a seating plan. This is the only way that you can ensure that guests who do not know anyone else do not end up sitting, for better or worse, next to your toothless, dilapidated great uncle. One of the very nicest things about the anticipation of a wedding is the number of old friends you are likely to meet up with or the nice people you will meet for the first time, with whom you will have something in common.

Brides should avoid the natural temptation to try to enforce an unnatural mix of the generations. People are really better with their own age groups and this applies to the older as well as the younger generations. Meals can seem to drag on if you are not involved in lively conversation. However much your old schoolfriend tries, there are a limited number of subjects she will probably find to discuss with your elderly relatives. Once the niceties of small talk are over, a deathly quiet can fall. This is the last thing you want at your wedding reception.

A good way to start off the table allocation is to look down the list of positive replies and pick a really solid, extrovert couple for each table. Next, isolate all those who will be attending alone or will not know many people and include them at this stage and with a view to putting them next to someone who will take responsibility for involving them in the general conversation. Do not leave them as fillers at the end. After you have done this, the tables are much easier to fill up. Think about interests people might share – sporting or professional. Do they have children the same age? That is always a good place to start.

Make sure that at least one copy of the seating plan is displayed clearly during the early part of the reception. Guests can be listed in alphabetical order with the number of the table at which they are sitting next to the names. Alternatively, table numbers or letters (and make sure you know which your caterer or hotel uses – numbers or letters) can be listed as headings, with the group of guests at each detailed underneath. So long as a table plan is legible and neat, it can be as simple as you like. When guests are called to sit down by the toast-master, banqueting manager or best man, make sure someone is posted in a prominent position to help anyone find their place.

Brides and grooms may choose to take their seats last, in which case the assembled guests may applaud them to their seats. The top table is always served first, to allow guests to commence eating as soon as they have their food and avoid their having to wait for their hosts, as politeness would expect.

If you were a wedding guest facing the top table and the bridal party were facing you, the traditional seating order from left to right would be:

Chief Bridesmaid/Groom's Father/Brides's Mother/Groom/ Bride/Bride's Father/Groom's Mother/Best Man

Little bridesmaids old enough to sit still may be added on to either end, if desired.

In the case of step-parents, unless the stepmother or stepfather has brought the child up, and to all intents and purposes has replaced the original parent, they would not be seated at the top table. Second husbands and wives do not play a big part at the weddings of the children from the first marriage. If the original parent is still living and is planning to attend the wedding, their presence at a formal top table should be considered, even in the case of very estranged families. If a step-parent is to be included on the top table as well as the original parent, the original parent should be encouraged to provide an escort as balance. The more people you include on the top table, the more space it will take up. Top tables will only have the families sitting on one side, facing the guests. If you have a particularly large family and would like to seat members of the family opposite you on the top table, remember that it will need to be wider than the normal single trestle table width used for top tables.

Close family should be placed at tables close to the top table, as should the older guests, out of respect. Younger friends of the couple would normally be pushed a little further away in favour of this principle. Given that your close friends will probably be so busy gossiping and enjoying themselves (male and female alike), they are unlikely to notice the position of their table. For this reason, younger friends will help to bolster up the boundaries of the reception space and ensure that conversation does not dwindle as you move further away from the centre of the action. If any friends are likely to be offended by being at the furthest table, you ought to just pre-warn them, explaining that it is just because you consider your bond of friendship to be so strong, you feel that you can ask for their support in this manner.

Married couples and those in an established relationship would normally be placed at the same table. Unless recently married (given to be within one year) or in a very new or young relationship, couples do not sit next to each other. It is nice to have a fair mix of men and women at each table, if at all possible.

# CHAPTER 7
# Preserving Wedding Gowns and Bouquets

## 1. Gowns

Unless you are planning to have your wedding dress altered after the wedding so that you will be able to wear it again, it is likely that it will simply live out the rest of its life in a wardrobe somewhere. This life could well be relatively short unless you take steps to ensure the survival of the fabric and colours and prevent dust getting into the cloth and yellowing the fabric. It is not surprising that gown preservation is becoming more and more popular and the number of companies offering this service is increasing. The process will normally involve a thorough cleaning of the dress and restoration to the best degree achievable, followed by treatment with a special solution to prevent ageing and subsequent packing in a sealed box. It must be remembered, however, that any stains suffered by the dress during the wedding should be removed as soon as possible, even if you are planning to have the dress professionally preserved at a later date. Wedding gown preservation means that if at some time in the future you have a daughter or even granddaughter who might like to wear your wedding dress, it will still be an option. There is no guarantee that the dress will survive without proper preservation. The cost of professional preservation is minimal in comparison to the cost of the average wedding dress and well worth the investment. Other clothing – veils, headdresses etc. – can also be treated in the same way.

## 2. Bouquets

Bridal bouquets have a special significance for many women. Even if they have thrown their bouquet during the reception, they may well wish to retrieve it in order to have it preserved in some way. There are a variety of options.

Flowers can be pressed and framed to make attractive pictures with a nostalgic element, following a romantic tradition greatly favoured by the Victorians. Bouquets can also be dried whole and covered under glass for protection. Many talented florists and dried-flower artists offer these services. You could also have a go at preserving your own bouquet if you would prefer this. If you would like to try to do this, it would be best to have at least one practice session with unimportant flowers just to get the technique right.

You will need to buy enough Silica Gel crystals to produce sufficient powder when ground down to dust each flower and leaf individually. It can be quite expensive, so practice will ensure that you buy the right amount. It is sold in most large chemists. Silica Gel absorbs water content and is most commonly used in packaging and between the panes of double glazed windows. Used for preserving flowers, Silica Gel will protect the colour and form in a way that is not really achievable through ordinary airdrying.

1. Grind the crystals down to a fine powder in a food processor or pestle and mortar. Make sure that you only do this in a well-ventilated room, since the dust is most unpleasant if taken into the mouth. If possible, wear some sort of mask for protection otherwise you may well have the driest mouth you have ever experienced.
2. Using a clean, dry, soft brush, such as a paintbrush, carefully coat each flower petal and leaf with the powder until every part is covered.
3. Place in an airtight container and fill up with remaining powder, completely covering the flowers if possible.
4. Seal and leave in a warm place for one week.
5. Gently remove flowers from the powder and spray with an artist's fixative spray or even a fine hairspray. Allow to dry naturally.
6. Treat the preserved flowers with care – they will be brittle and will break easily. If possible, cover with glass.

Remember that the earlier you treat any flower with Silica Gel powder, the better. The fresher the flower, the better the finished preserved state.

# CHAPTER 8
# Touching Base

## 1. Responsibilities as a couple

Having concerned yourself with the activities and responsibilities of the wedding team, you must give yourself time to sit down quietly with your fiancé to go over various points. You will certainly want to discuss your personal itineraries. You should also be very aware that in the lead up to the wedding brides and grooms often manage to see comparatively little of each other. You may need to go over arrangements for the honeymoon and essential items you might need to take. With your minds focused on the wedding for so long, other matters may have slipped a little. Think about getting bills paid before you disappear, cancelling the milk and other domestic matters.

One extremely important point for each of you to consider is the making of a will. It is a serious matter and should not be ignored just because it is probably the furthest thing from your minds. Marriage is all about responsibility and partnership. Having to face the fact that tragedy does exist at a time when you are focusing on the happy things in life is not easy. The making of a will is a duty you should each accept out of the love you share for each other.

## 2. Parental recognition

All through our lives, our parents care for us and support us, making every effort to ensure that we grow up to be responsible, well-mannered and balanced adults. Your wedding is likely to stir up memories of ages past, of your childhood and early achievements. They know that when you get married they are not really losing a child, but the emotions they feel can be quite overwhelming at times. You must remember the symbolic attachment your parents will have made to the fact of your marriage and be sensitive to the reasons behind what will often seem as unreasonable or irrational behaviour. In simple human terms, they have done their best by you and it will be quite an achievement. Hard work deserves recognition. In all your hurry and excitement, spare a thought for your parents and remember to keep a little time back to tell them how

grateful you are and how much you love them. No one can last
forever and the bond between you will only be strengthened by
your deliberate effort to give them cause for pride in you. Do
try to think about leaving some little gift, or even a short letter
for them to find after it is all over and the last family member
has gone. If the discovery prompts immediate and inevitable
tears, at least you know that they will be tears of joy.

# CHAPTER 9
# The Last 24 Hours

And so, the day is about to dawn. Only twenty-four short hours are left. Plan them with care so that you are occupied, but relaxed, finishing off honeymoon packing, having a manicure, perhaps arranging to spend a couple of quiet hours with a few friends. The tradition is that the bride and groom do not see each other on the day of the wedding until they meet at the ceremony. The chief bridesmaid will normally spend the night with the bride, as the best man will normally spend the night with the groom, partly to keep them calm, partly for companionship. Many more brides do get a good, peaceful night's sleep than they think they will. Perhaps the nervous excitement is enough to send them to sleep. Don't fall into the trap of staying up late, hoping to feel sleepy. Even just lying quietly in bed will be better for you than sitting up reading or talking. Try to centre your thoughts on your fiancé and how much you are looking forward to the most significant meeting of your life since the day you met.

There is no reason why you may not telephone the groom on the morning of the wedding. He is probably just as nervous as you and with all the stiff upper lip men seem to think they have to show, he will probably not find the relief for his nerves in words in the same way as you. He is really the one on the stage to begin with, as he waits for you to come. A brief, reassuring telephone call from you, or receiving a little gift you have thoughtfully sent round, will be just enough to give his confidence a boost. This is probably the most romantic telephone call you will ever share and one of the most fleeting opportunities.

Remember this little ancient superstition, as you leave for the ceremony, and glance approvingly at your reflection, feeling in control of your life and your choice to marry. Leave one item of your apparel off, as you look at yourself for the last time before leaving. No bride should ever see her full, complete appearance – pop the last little delicate bridal slipper on your foot and don't look back, this is your very own fairy tale.

# Contributors' Addresses

**Jacqueline Llewelyn Weddings Limited**
Registered Office:
Newgate House
431 London Road
London CR0 3PF
Tel 0181 665 7710

**Abercrombie and Kent**
Sloane Square House
Holbein Place
London SW1W 8NS
Tel 0171 730 9600

**The Admirable Crichton Limited**
Unit 5, Camberwell Trading Estate
Denmark Road
London SE5 9LB
Tel 0171 733 8113

**Detta Phillips**
22a Prince of Wales Mansions
Prince of Wales Drive
London SW11 4BQ
Tel 0171 498 2728

**Jacques Azagury**
50 Knightsbridge
London SW1X 7JN
Tel 0171 235 0799

**William Bartholomew**
18 The Talina Centre
Bagley's Lane
London SW6 2BW
Tel 0171 731 8328

**The Cottage Caterers Limited**
14 Manfield Park
Guildford Road
Cranleigh
Surrey GU6 8PT
Tel 01483 268326

**Fleetwood Limousines**
106 Gifford Street
London N1 0DF
Tel 0171 624 0869

**Gorgeous Gourmets**
Gresham Way
Wimbledon
London SW19 8ED
Tel 0181 944 7771

**Inside Outside Marquee Hire**
Unit 12, Bookham Industrial Park
Church Road
Great Bookham
Surrey KT23 3JT
Tel 01372 459485

**Zandra Rhodes**
85 Richford Street
London W6 7HJ
Tel 0181 749 3216

**Searcy's**
124 Bolingbroke Grove
London SW11 1DA
Tel 0171 585 0505
30 Pavilion Road
London SW1X 0HJ
Tel 0171 823 9212

# CONTRIBUTORS' ADDRESSES 271

**Ivor Spencer**
The Guild of Professional
    Toast-masters
12 Little Bornes
London SE21 8SE
Tel 0181 670 5585

**Vivienne Westwood**
6 Davies Street
London W1Y 1LJ
Tel 0171 629 3757

**The Wren Press**
26 Chelsea Wharf
15 Lots Road
London SW10 0QJ
Tel 0171 351 5887

# Index